LANDED

—— ❖ ——

TRANSFORMATIVE STORIES OF
CANADIAN IMMIGRANT WOMEN

GAYATHRI SHUKLA
WITH ELENA ESINA

ISBN: 9798832755397

www.campfirekinship.com

Cover art by Cynthia Cabrera.

Editing by Lindy Pfeil.

This book reflects the authors' present recollections of experiences over time. Occasionally, some names and characteristics have been changed to protect the identities of those mentioned. The views of the authors do not necessarily represent the views of Campfire Kinship Storytelling Inc.

In the spirit of respect, reciprocity and truth, we acknowledge that we live, work and play on the traditional territories of the Blackfoot Confederacy (Siksika, Kainai, Piikani), the Tsuut'ina, the Îyâxe Nakoda Nations, the Métis Nation (Region 3), and all people who make their homes in the Treaty 7 region of Southern Alberta.

From Gayathri
To my parents, Malathi and Srini, for braving the journey of immigration, and gifting me with both roots and wings.

From Elena
To my son, Lev, for inspiring me to make the life changes that open doors. May you boldly walk through them!

CONTENTS

A Message from the Lieutenant Governor of Alberta

Growing up in East Africa, I learned about Ubuntu, a Bantu word that simply translated means, "I am because we are." It speaks to the interconnected nature of humanity and tells us that we are all linked in our trials and tribulations, and in our successes and our opportunities. Here in Canada we are bound by a similar covenant as partners in a fundamental treaty relationship that is an ongoing, living agreement between peoples. Working through the essential process of truth and reconciliation, caring for the precious land we share, and helping one another to succeed are collective responsibilities.

My husband and I began our journey as settlers here in the late 1970s. We arrived as stateless persons, following the expulsion of all citizens of South Asian heritage from our native Uganda. While we have been blessed with support and opportunities to build a good life and to give back, there were initial feelings of trepidation and loneliness that came with making such a momentous change. I have met countless immigrant women who have shared these feelings, and so many of them have surmounted far more daunting obstacles in building a new life than what we faced.

I have also been privileged to meet inspiring and fearless women who have persevered in their dreams to forge a path that allows them to share their distinct voice and abilities in meaningful ways. The work often begins at the grassroots. They see a need or an opportunity and start where they are, with whatever they have at hand. They find a way to learn from their challenges and to convert those experiences into positive actions. Even the smallest step, when taken with thought and resolve, will propel you forward.

I offer my heartfelt thanks to the women sharing their stories in this anthology, and to Gayathri Shukla and Elena Esina for encouraging them to do so with strength and candor. Each of the journeys chronicled here speaks to the fact that we share so many common dreams and goals, despite the outward differences that may appear to set us apart. Collectively, these stories show us that we all hold the power to lift up those around us. Ultimately, the success of our society as a whole depends on the understanding and opportunities we are each afforded to flourish. We all belong, we have our own gifts to share, and there is room in our communities for everyone to thrive.

Her Honour, the Honourable Salma Lakhani
AOE, B.Sc., LLD (hon)
Lieutenant Governor of Alberta

FOREWORD

I grew up in a country where I wasn't an immigrant, but I was constantly asked the dreaded "Where are you from?" question. After immigrating to Canada at age 17, people still asked me that question, but becoming an immigrant was a relief: I was no longer "othered" in the place I was actually from.

I had moved to Canada from Australia in the winter of 1995. In my first year in Canada, I worked a retail job and frequently told people that I was half Indian and played hockey. At 5′3″ I looked like a gust of wind could blow me away, and people would look at me and say, "really?"...I didn't realize they thought I was an Indigenous ice hockey player with an Australian accent.

What I meant was that I grew up listening to my parents play Lata Mangeshkar, stealing papadams from my dad's Indian restaurant, and making huge divots in my backyard with a field hockey stick while kangaroos hopped on by (ok, everything was true except that last part).

As an immigrant, I'm still learning 27 years later. The loss of a sense of shared cultural identity has been hard. The loss of an understanding of where 'home' is. The feeling that no one else in the world truly 'gets' my cultural identity and therefore gets me (a feeling exacerbated by being multiracial). At moments, I celebrate being unique; while at other times, I feel like an outlier, an anomaly.

The places we have come from, the places we have moved to, and the places we will go shape our relationships, our experiences, our lives. They shape who we are. And the reality is, unless we are Indigenous, we are all immigrants.

But my story of moving from one country to another was a fortunate one. I can't claim to have confronted the magnitude of challenges that many immigrants face - a process that can take a lifetime. I wasn't displaced from my country. I didn't flee war or natural disaster. I came by choice and was privileged as a legal, documented, young immigrant. I could already speak the language of my new country. While Canadians often told me that I didn't look Australian, my lighter skin and "cool" Australian accent made things easier for me.

Sharing my story and hearing others' stories has been a balm for my heart. I have come to realize that the feeling of not belonging is an inherent part of the human experience. And strangely, through that recognition, I feel a sense of belonging with all the people who have ever not belonged.

In 2016, I co-founded an organization called Humainologie. Gathering and sharing human stories has been at the center of our work. In 2020, I met Gayathri and we connected on our shared belief in the power of storytelling to empower people and create empathy. She had just started Campfire Kinship and organized an event for Humainologie's Empathy Week. She brought together a diverse group of individuals to share career stories that revealed resilience and kindness.

Since then, Gayathri and her team have featured hundreds of stories through their Instagram platform (@campfire_kinship), as well as their video storytelling project *unLikely Friends*, podcast *Hearth 2 Heart*, and other media publications. Campfire Kinship's training programs, storytelling workshops, and strategic advisory have already helped thousands of employees and leaders to celebrate diversity and build a more inclusive workplace. And we've been meaningful collaborators ever since Empathy Week.

The stories in this book are heartfelt, sometimes heartbreaking, vulnerable, powerful, meaningful, and true. I convey my deep respect to each of the authors. It can take heroic authenticity to share our personal journeys which are too often marked by hardship, exclusion, pain, and shame as immigrants.

I hope that some pain and shame can be freed through sharing stories. I hope that by pointing to systems of exclusion that don't serve the world, these stories help dismantle those systems. I hope that the magnificence of the voices in this book is recognized, valued, and celebrated. Finally, I hope that together, as readers and storytellers, we find refuge and connection in our fragile, complex, and beautiful shared humanity.

Salima Stanley-Bhanji (she/her), CEO, Humainologie

INTRODUCTION

GAYATHRI SHUKLA

"You're a foreigner!"

I was at a meeting in downtown Calgary when those words stopped me in my tracks.

I stared in disbelief at the person who uttered them. "Are you talking to me?"

"Yes, you. You're a foreigner!"

Before I could respond, the person on my right spoke up: "If she's a foreigner, I am one too. I was born in Australia."

"So am I. I was born in England," the person on my left quipped.

A few tense moments passed.

Finally, he tried to justify his original comment: "Well, I was born in Canada, but I am not Indigenous, so technically, that makes me a foreigner too!"

More awkward silence.

"Sorry, bad joke. Let's get on with the meeting," he stammered through a nervous laugh.

The meeting carried on, and we never spoke of the incident again. But in the days and weeks afterward, questions played out in my mind in an endless loop:

Do any of us have a right to belong, given that we reside on stolen Indigenous land? Was it really a joke or was I singled out because of my race? (Three out of four of us in that room were born outside Canada, but I was the only person of color.) More perplexingly, how would I have responded had my peers not graciously stepped in?

Today, I have (some) answers.

First, yes, immigrants belong. But whether our families immigrated last month or a century back, we are all still newcomers. As newcomers, we must acknowledge the original stewards of Turtle Island - the First Nations, Métis, and Inuit people; the harms that forcibly excluded Indigenous peoples from their ancestry, the impacts of which are still perpetuated today. We each must endeavor to break the cycle of violence and harm.

Second, it's not a joke to call an immigrant a foreigner. Dictionaries assign 'foreigner' with synonyms like imposter and outsider. Too often, immigrants face biases and stigmas that perpetually alienate us from our adopted homes. Anti-immigrant sentiment has been exacerbated in recent times, with a disturbing rise seen with anti-Black and anti-Asian hate crimes, to name just two. However, Canada depends on immigration to achieve economic prosperity. In other words, due to factors like declining fertility rates and an aging population, Canada *needs* immigration to fill the gaps in its labor force. As per the Government of Canada's 2020 estimate, immigrants are expected to represent up to 30% of Canada's population by 2036 (www.canada.ca).

We may each look and sound different, but our diversity turns the fabric of multicultural Canada into a vibrant tapestry.

But first I must tell the story of how this book came to be. It all started over a coffee with my friend, Elena Esina. We initially met as board directors at the Calgary Immigrant Women's Association. We both fervently felt that immigrant women add tremendous value to Canadian society, but these stories often went untold.

I shared with Elena that I had recently been certified in guided autobiography, an evidence-based method of writing and sharing life stories in a supportive group setting. I had started to embed storytelling in my company, Campfire Kinship's inclusion and diversity programs, and I wanted to do more in the community. Elena mentioned her experience in project management and that she was interested in the creative non-fiction writing process, as the bulk of her writing was for academic projects at the University of Calgary. Our experiences combined with a mutual desire to give voice to immigrant stories sparked an idea: why not write a book shedding light on the lived experiences of immigrant women?

I applied for a grant to Calgary Arts Development. To my excitement, it was approved, and our project was born! Elena joined me as the project manager and her steadfast support has been a blessing ever since. We organized a call for applications from local first- and second-generation immigrant women and gender non-conforming folks. It received an overwhelming amount of interest.

We gathered virtually with successful applicants for the first time in early 2022, and I facilitated a series of workshops using guided autobiography. Thus began the intricate process of unearthing our stories from within our hearts and getting them out on paper. From reflective exercises to multiple rounds of group readings, and editing, the stories in this book came to fruition through a collaborative labor of love. Our countries of origin include Afghanistan, Australia, Bangladesh, Brazil, Cameroon, Canada, China, Chile, England, Fiji, French Polynesia, Hong Kong, India, Japan, Kazakhstan, Kenya, Malaysia, Mexico, Myanmar, Pakistan, Philippines, Russia, Saudi Arabia, Singapore, Slovenia, South Africa, Turkey, Ukraine, United Arab Emirates, and Vietnam.

As you'll see in these pages, each voice tells a unique tale of overcoming adversity, in some cases even having to flee war and violence to find a better future. And yet, each voice is a beautiful testament to grit, contribution, and transformation.

Personally, the process put into sharp focus how much I am grateful for our home – Canada! Does this mean we have a fully inclusive society? No, we aren't there yet. The foreigner sentiment is just one example of biases that immigrants navigate. But we cannot take for granted the freedoms we enjoy, such as democracy and peace. We are standing on the shoulders of those who fought hard to gain us these rights, and especially women's rights.

This brings me back to the foreigner comment – and how I would have responded.

Truthfully, the easy response is one of anger. A few choice words and phrases come to mind. ("Put 'em in their place," as they say. I imagine it would have felt quite satisfying at the moment.)

But as I write these words today, I realize that, while anger is a default reaction, there's no point if it fails to build a bridge and further drives a polarizing wedge. Isn't entrenchment in 'us versus them' at the root of division, discrimination, and dehumanization?

So, after much reflection, I choose to put forth an invitation instead, in the form of this book. Not just for the person who mistakenly called me a foreigner but for every person who has ever wondered: what is it like to be an immigrant?

Enclosed in this book are 37 authentic stories that illuminate what it means to give up everything you knew, and embrace your new home despite the stigmas and obstacles. We hope it will pique your curiosity to walk in the shoes of those who identify as immigrants. Curiosity is the fuel for understanding, connection, and empathy. Without it, we are all prone to making snap judgments, which is the fuel for stereotypes, fear, and separation. So, give yourself the permission to remain curious and suspend judgment. Read the stories one at a time. Sit with the emotions that arise, even if they feel uncomfortable. Look things up that are unfamiliar. Stay open to a courageous conversation about differences.

And if you identify as an immigrant – we believe this applies to you too. Whether you just arrived in Canada or have established your roots, we hope you'll see yourself reflected in these pages and find inspiration to persevere in this journey to belong.

1

BECOMING THE PERSON I'VE ALWAYS BEEN

ADO NKEMKA

I turn 30 this February and I'm just starting to feel like I belong.

I always felt as though life was harder than it needed to be, and school – at least in the early years – was my escape.

In kindergarten, I faced anti-Black racism for the first time – that I'm aware of, of course. One boy told me I couldn't hang out with the class during lunch. So, I spent many lunches alone at a school in Québec ironically called École Des Nations. That was just the beginning of my experience of being racially othered.

For the most part, grades 2 to 5 at École Félix Leclerc were fun. It wasn't until I moved to Île-Perrot, a 45-minute drive from Montréal, that I truly understood that I was Black.

Côte-des-Neiges is a multicultural area of Montréal. There, I always knew I was an immigrant amongst other immigrants, and so, despite being Black, I didn't feel like I didn't belong. While the lunch time experience had been sad, it didn't scare me or leave me with a complex about my race. But when we moved into a predominantly white area, my self-concept changed completely.

1

In Île-Perrot, I felt simultaneously invisible and hyper-visible. I experienced being the subject of bias – that thing I could feel without being able to speak it, or theorize it, or place it within a greater historical context. That was when I started internalizing my inferiority and finding ways to fit into whiteness.

In 2006, my family moved to the northeast of Calgary, Alberta. Despite its multiculturalism, I soon realized that everyone was anti-Black - including fellow persons of color and my own white friends. I've resented the fact that white and non-Black immigrants had an easier time assimilating than I did. It seemed like no matter how socialized as a Canadian – or North American – I was, I was constantly reminded that my skin color makes me an outsider. And the darker your skin, especially as a woman, the less access and warm welcomes you receive.

At 29, I accepted that I'll never know what it's like to be stressed to the brink as a parent. And my own parents will never understand what it's like to grow up not feeling good enough at home, or out in this Western world.

Growing up, I had a dream. That dream was to be a singer. I internalized my inferiority, and my insecurity didn't allow me to pursue this dream wholeheartedly. At home, singing was never encouraged as a viable career path. Dark skin wasn't – and still isn't – wholeheartedly valued by the media.

After high school, I went straight into post-secondary. Then left. Then returned. You get the picture. I felt like music was out of reach, but my heart was never into "sensible" pursuits. I figured sociology would be the easiest way to get a degree. I needed a safe educational space.

After ignoring the world's racism and my own internalized racism for too long, I finally reached a point where I couldn't laugh it off anymore. I needed a space where I could openly and honestly discuss race and other social issues. I needed to face the reality that under our current social constructs, not all humans are equal.

Leading up to graduation, my student loan felt overwhelming: the result of indecisive overspending and coping with a damaged spirit. The idea of repayment was (and still is) incredibly stressful.

One day, my mom told me she had 20K set aside for me.

I think immigrant parents, specifically Black/Africans, don't recognize the struggle of being a first-generation immigrant. They left their countries for economic prosperity in the Western world and assume their children – raised in Canada – have it easier. They don't realize that first-generation immigrants experience consistent racialization, which impacts their self-worth at a very young age.

They come here and work hard, and they may think that responsible parenting means not "handing anything to you." But they forget that they did not spend their childhood sticking out like a sore thumb, at least not based on race – one of many things you can't change.

At 29, I'm finally making money in music, through teaching. I want to build a career selling my art and connecting to a crowd, but now, at least I can say I've found my will to live again.

What I would tell my younger self is that while resilience is a word that is starting to lose favor in the social justice world, the truth is, you're going to need it. You're going to come across a lot of people who see you as an outsider. To get to where you want to be, you're going to need self-assurance, because people are going to project onto you their ideas of what your life should look like. Only you know what you want. Don't let them dim your brilliance.

They say you're going to have to work twice as hard. Just work hard. You won't be able to do this alone. Rely on your intuition and invite the right people into your life. Find the answers to your questions. Apply the knowledge. Be consistent. One day you'll realize you're living a whole new life – one where you're honored, even if you're the only one honoring yourself.

But you won't be alone, you'll find people who'll want to help you along the way.

2

A Little Girl Dreams

Adriana Sartori

I'm Adriana and I'm 50 years old. Not a little girl anymore, but I still have that little girl's dreams.

I was born on a small coffee farm in the Brazilian countryside to a single mother, and my mother and I lived with my grandparents. They were immigrants themselves, having moved from Italy to Brazil after the First World War. We were poor but I was happy, and my mom was a loving mom.

My biggest dream as a little girl was to go to school and become a cashier at the village grocery shop. I used to go there with my mom on horseback. I can still taste the dulce de leche the owner used to give me.

When I was eight, my mom got pregnant again. I was not yet in school because it was too far away. One of my mom's sisters came to visit and decided to take me with her to Rio de Janeiro, so that I could attend school. My heart was broken but at the same time full of hope. I was finally going to school, but I would be separated from my mom.

At age 26, after many years of dedication, work, and study, I became a physiotherapist with a master's in neurological conditions. I was so proud. At 28, I married a fellow physiotherapist, and we opened our own practice. This meant 12-hour workdays, with a two-hour daily commute in traffic. We barely made enough to pay the bills.

In 2008, we discovered that Canada was open for skilled workers and physiotherapy was on the list. We immigrated in 2009, in the middle of winter, with $4,000 and four pieces of luggage. I was afraid and sad about leaving my mom behind. But I was also excited about the future.

After landing in Vancouver, we both worked in retail and started the process of becoming Canadian licensed physiotherapists. But it was so expensive that we could only afford for one of us to do this.

Years of paperwork and translations later, I finally passed the written exam and could work as a physio. By this time, we were living in Calgary, and I was also teaching Pilates. With only the practical exam to pass, I could not have been happier.

In 2017, when I failed the practical a second time, I decided to dedicate 100% of my time to the exam. I cut down on time spent at work, leisure, on the house and with my husband. This was my last chance. For almost three months I vomited daily and lost six kilograms. People started asking what was wrong, and I was diagnosed with anxiety and depression.

Despite working in a Canadian clinic for more than a year, I failed the practical exam a third and final time: I could not try again. I was so surprised. I had been one of the best in my study group and I was so sure about my answers. My manager had been ready to hire me full time and raise my wage. She had told me, "I can't lose someone like you."

My score was more than 100 points above average. So how had I failed?

It transpired that the certifying body has a "subjective" part of the score. This means that the person observing your practical has the right to judge you subjectively. I was judged to be unprofessional with three of the 16 stations or "patients" (they are actors), not listening to their concerns, putting three of them at risk for injury. I was also deemed condescending towards one of my "patients."

I was, of course, shocked.

After emails, appeals, letters from my patients and manager, I received a call: "Sorry, if you had been to a Canadian school, we could reconsider."

I asked for recordings, but there were none.

I was devastated. One person's judgement had destroyed all my dreams. My hard work and the $30,000 spent to get to the final exam – all wasted. I lost my job at the clinic as they could not keep anyone after failing the exam a third time.

The hardest part was leaving the clinic, walking out of reception, past all my clients waiting for me to take away their pain. I drove home crying, screaming and angry. I knew I was a good physiotherapist. But what could I do? I could no longer hang my diploma on the wall. My world had collapsed.

After praying one day, I opened my Bible. In 2 Corinthians 4:8 it says, "We are troubled on every side, yet not distressed; we are perplexed, but not in despair; persecuted, but not forsaken; cast down, but not destroyed." This felt like a wakeup call from God.

After mourning for a couple of months, my husband and I opened our own Pilates studio. It has been very successful, even during the pandemic. I'm my own boss. I still teach people how to move better, how to achieve their physical goals and how to manage their bodies if they have any physical impairment.

My younger self had no idea that her dream of becoming a cashier would bring her this far. Now I dream about retiring to a ranch and perhaps working in the village grocery store as a cashier a couple of times a week, to meet people and share a smile.

In the words of Joshua 1:9, "I repeat, be strong and brave! Don't be afraid and don't panic, for I, the LORD your God, am with you in all you do."

3

A JOURNEY TO CULTIVATING INNER PEACE

AMEN KAUR

C algary winters in the early '90s could be brutal. Bundled head to toe, with only my eyes peeping through the layers, I would walk slowly to school through knee-high snow. The mornings were dark, and a windy chill howled through the dreadful emptiness that accompanied me each day.

School wasn't a choice: every kid had to go. So, I would put on a brave face and stomp through the white field with my two little siblings. We would imagine we were lost in the Arctic. School was where we would find other humans, even if they weren't kind.

Calgary is my birth city, the only home I had ever known, but I never felt accepted. And I was always a target. One day as we were setting off for school, my neighbor yelled after her kids: "One of you hold her. The other kick her in the stomach!"

My heart dropped. I felt sick to my stomach. But it was a feeling I was used to, so I pushed it aside and kept walking. By that point, I'd heard the racial slur, "Paki," more times than I could count, though for years I didn't know what it meant. You see, there weren't very many of us around. Back

9

then, the handful of Punjabi families in the city all knew each other.

My parents emigrated from Punjab, India in the '70s. My father, a hardworking man whose life revolved around providing for his family, didn't have time for my tears. My mother was my haven. She would listen and offer compassion. That's all she had the strength for. I quickly learned that as a woman, her role was limited and as a child, so was my voice.

So often, sharing the horrors I experienced outside the home was met with calls to "toughen up." I get it. It was hard for immigrants: a new language, extreme weather, big responsibilities. So different from the life they'd left behind. They had to "toughen up" to survive, so I was expected to do the same. Besides, upsetting the "head of the house" would often result in memorable methods of discipline towards us kids. Children were meant to be "kept in line." It was a rulebook written by the generations before and given to the next to carry out.

I endured the pain quietly and alone.

All this time, I had been learning to call on the universe for strength. When I needed protection or felt lonely and unloved, it was always there. My parents relied deeply on this power in their meditation practice. They spoke of an energy that permeated nature and lived in every heart. I figured out how to access it in my own way. There, I started to find belonging and empowerment.

By the mid '90s, I was in junior high and connected with a group of friends – all minorities. For the first time I felt sisterhood. It was incredible. Suddenly, I wasn't the magnet who attracted bullies. The first time I heard whispers of someone having a crush on me, I was shocked and scared, but welcomed the warm feeling of acceptance.

I came home from school one day to learn that we were moving. Not to a different city, but a different country. To India. Questioning our elders wasn't allowed, so I tried reassuring myself, hoping maybe this would be for the best. I was completely unaware of how much life was about to change.

I landed in a country buzzing with people coming out of every corner. In summer, it was so hot that I could feel every drop of sweat under my clothes. Vehicles beeped constantly and the warm wind blew dust into my eyes.

My stomach would be in knots every morning as I donned my uniform and headed to Catholic school, a place where the kids stared at me as if I were an alien and mocked my Canadian English accent. Teachers had full authority to punish kids through physical means whenever they pleased.

Each day, 3 p.m. couldn't come soon enough. I grabbed my siblings, strapping one to the back of my bike, and pedaled home as fast as I could. I kept my furrowed brow firm for the entire 45-minute ride so that all the men who stared or whistled at me, would question their choice. To think I feared these strangers more than the older men called relatives. At least on a bike I could get away. At a relative's home, I was a sitting duck to unsolicited attention.

Sometimes, I just wanted to go outside and play badminton with the neighborhood kids. I learned that, as a girl, it was better to focus on household tasks or homework instead. As I became quieter on the outside, I became louder on the inside, and my frustration knew no bounds. Uncomfortable summer nights were spent secretly shedding tears, praying to this higher power to take me home.

As a teenage girl, it felt like prison. I channeled my angst towards my studies. In two years, I learned two languages and figured out how to feel comfortable conforming and fitting in. Sure, it meant dimming my light, but I understood what I needed to do to get by.

Four years after landing in India, I returned to Canada to complete high school. It meant living with relatives in B.C. until my family was able to move back. I was thrilled but terrified. This was high school, and I didn't know the people I was living with. I remember hiding under my bed in the dark, hyperventilating as I listened to yelling. I lived there for a year, and during that time I witnessed many things I didn't understand.

I channeled my confusion and sorrow into academics. Every day I sought courage from my inner light to study hard enough to complete grades 11 and 12 in one year. I had great interactions with the kids and teachers in high school, but nothing so memorable that I wasn't happy to graduate.

This was the freedom I'd been waiting for, for so long. I had a post-secondary plan and delved deeper into my spiritual practice. The deeper I went, the more empowered and connected to the universe I became.

Music would elevate me into a state of love I had never experienced before. A love much bigger than relationships. I couldn't tell if it was my imagination or reality. It was as if I knew how to move with the wind, as if nature spoke to me. I couldn't stop myself from dancing in the rain.

The more joy I felt from this shift, the more my heart went towards it, and the less pain and suffering I found. My imagination began shifting into reality. Through it, manifested a great love of a partner in life, the power to set boundaries and a voice with which to make decisions. As a proud Canadian Sikh woman who felt protected and safe in her homeland –a country where I felt I could express myself without fear, nothing could hold me back from embracing my individuality and sovereignty.

When life finally graced me with motherhood, I made a promise to my rainbow child to try my hardest to do better as a parent. To end harmful intergenerational cycles. To recognize the hypocrisies within me and parent authentically. To listen with an open heart and give my child a voice so he could always feel powerful. To treat him with respect so he grows up knowing his value and how to treat others. To love him unconditionally so he knows he can come to me with any feeling, and it would always be accepted. To know the power of connection within himself so he never feels alone.

I will make plenty of mistakes along the way as I unlearn harmful patterns. Healing is a process. And I am deeply grateful for the sacrifices made by my parents because it's no longer about survival. It's time to take what I've learned and evolve so the next generation can thrive.

Life taught me how to move through pain and transform it into power. My journey so far, pulled a warrior out of me. Nature taught me how to reach for a deep inner love, a love I hope to embody one day. My journey showed me the way to healing, peace within, and how to manifest the life I want. How to romanticize hope even in dark times. This pain served as a catalyst to share with others, through my Instagram parenting blog and books as an author, a way of love that heals.

I look forward to how the remainder of my story unfolds.

4

THE DUSKY DAWN

ANAM KAZIM

I n my early teens in Karachi, Pakistan, the fire within me was full-blown. I aimed to pursue my ambitions, and excel in all areas of my life, through continuous learning and education. My goal was to be an all-rounder, appreciating the value and purpose of everything in life. I always believed that it is education that opens our minds and helps us to be the best versions of ourselves: a seashell that encompasses us like a water droplet and transforms us into a pearl.

Higher education is expensive in Pakistan and not perceived as necessary for females. Instead, parents build their reputation upon the extravagance of their daughter's wedding. The never-ending recession and my burning desire for education, motivated my parents to immigrate to Canada. We landed in Toronto in December 2002, in the middle of a snowstorm. But it was a moment of warmth for me, as I felt closer to my dream of a higher education. I happily accepted the challenges of settling in a new country with its own customs and norms. There was extensive diversity in Toronto, and I felt welcomed by my high school teachers, staff, and students.

After high school, I pursued chemical engineering, something I had imagined doing at age 13, when I was living in rural Pakistan. I completed undergraduate and graduate degrees in chemical and environmental engineering at Western University in London, Ontario.

A year after finishing my graduate degree, I moved to Calgary to build a career in chemical engineering. It was like relocating to another country. As much as I was embraced in Ontario, regardless of race, gender, and religion, I was an outlander in Alberta. Moreover, when I experienced superficial kindness, I felt simply tolerated or unwelcome. Kindness feels void at the expense of one's own dignity. When one's dignity is compromised, one's identity is rejected.

I was excited to build relationships with colleagues, neighbors, and people in the community, and begin a new life in the new city. But my professional life was one of toxicity. On my team, I was the only female with an engineering background from a racialized community, new not only to the company, but also to Alberta, and all on my own. Hence, I was susceptible to the toxic corporate culture that enabled narcissism, bullying, misogyny, harassment, racism, and sexism. I was well-versed in conflict resolution, and defusing high-conflict situations, but I didn't know how to deal with narcissists. I persevered through the toxicity because my job meant everything to me.

I did find profoundly supportive friends in the organization. I will always cherish the stimulating conversations, the laughs, the lifting of spirits, and encouragement for each other's success. Their friendship was the lotus flower – purity that blossoms in the dirtiest waters. I am grateful because their presence gave me courage.

In the fall of 2014, Alberta experienced political and democratic flux. Protesters in downtown Calgary increased each day. Their rallies were an expression of anger towards the provincial government. Watching from my office, the restlessness inside me resonated with the chaos outside. The pain within me was great enough to give me the strength to partake in anything.

"Enough is enough," I said to myself. "I am running in the upcoming provincial elections as an NDP candidate." I joined Alberta's New Democratic Party, and promoted policies empowering marginalized groups, liberating educational institutions from self-serving entities, and putting people first. After all, our society exists because of the people.

History was made on the night of May 5, 2015, when Alberta's NDP formed government for the first time. My tie on election night with the Progressive Conservative Party candidate was unprecedented in Alberta. There were two rounds of vote recounts with Elections Alberta and an additional round in the court of justice, because the PC candidate challenged the recount outcome twice. I was officially announced as the winner and declared Member of the Legislative Assembly for Calgary-Glenmore, winning by only six votes (also unprecedented in Alberta).

It was a memorable experience to start a new chapter of my life with the hope of empowering our society by protecting human rights, and fostering equity, diversity, and inclusion. While I was dedicated to serving Albertans, and representing their best interests, I adhered to my values of respect, authenticity, empathy, fairness, and integrity in the face of hypocrisy, racism, bullying, manipulation and exclusion. In 2019, when I sought nomination to run again as the NDP candidate for Calgary-Glenmore, the opposing contestant defeated me and ran as the NDP candidate instead. My belief is that victory does not lie in the winning but in making a difference and I made that difference through my dedication. Therefore, I perceived that moment of my life as a door to new beginnings.

I embraced a life full of sweetness after politics, as I pursued my dream of running a honey and natural medicine business in the spring of 2019. It was beautiful to offer cures using apitherapy, aromatherapy and apothecary. As the business began to grow, the pandemic hit, which unveiled my potential to be resilient and to uphold integrity amid the business shutdown. As James Lane Allen notes, "Adversity does not build character, it reveals it."

Once I shut down my business, I focused on soul searching, and I was able to fully connect to myself. As a result, I designed a made-in-Alberta fragrance called INTRIGUE, inspired by the long, dark, extremely cold nights and aurora lights. The fragrance is a manifestation of my time in Alberta and an expression of my transformation, all infused in the form of a scent. I would like to acknowledge the mastery of Wildrose Perfumery Inc. in our Wildrose County for manufacturing the personalized perfume exactly the way I conceived it.

My time in Calgary has been filled with days that were both wild and rosy. I have learned, in the words of Imam Ali (A.S), to "be like a flower that gives its fragrance even to the hand that crushes it."

5

Two Suitcases

Anna Zakharova

W hen I was a little rural girl, daydreaming was one of my favorite pastimes. Whatever I heard or saw could make my thoughts fly far away. A thought-provoking trigger could be a teacher's question in a cold winter classroom, the song of a skylark in the hot summer sky while grazing village cows with dad, or eating a juicy peach from our garden and petting my dog (and best friend) Lusia. While pulling weeds at the carrot plantation with my family, I pictured myself walking across a green lawn of a western university campus hugging my books, just like the Beverly Hills TV show.

One day, walking home from the village school, I decided to walk through a small park instead of taking the usual sidewalk. I wondered, was it my choice which way to go, or was it already decided by God somewhere up there. I chose to go through the park thinking that I changed my fate by making a decision. Twenty years later, I was not so sure that my destiny was my own choice when my parents and I were fleeing our home on a last train to my sister in Canada and into uncertainty.

In early spring of 2014, foreign troops invaded Ukraine and occupied beautiful Crimea. A month later a war broke out in the east of Ukraine. At the time, I was not upset about leaving. Rather, I feared being detained by Russian paramilitary and tortured like the coordinator of our protest movement in Crimea. Or being found dead in a ditch like Reshat Ametov, a father of three who went on a one-man protest. After what Russia did in Transdniestria, Chechnya and Georgia, I knew that anything could be expected from Mr. Putin.

Russia invaded Crimea when the Ukrainian people were mourning the loss of over 100 civil protesters in Kyiv who were killed by the pro-Russian dictator Victor Yanukovych. Blue and yellow Ukrainian flags were the symbol of awakening of national identity and democratic aspirations. Russia's paramilitary in Crimea started to persecute people wearing these colors. So, I took off my blue and yellow ribbon bracelet and hid it along with my Ukrainian flag and the rest of my life that could fit into two suitcases.

After a few hours of travelling in silence we saw Ukrainian flags at the "border" with the mainland Ukraine. The whirlpool of adrenalin in my stomach turned into tears of relief that we were now safe. This was mixed with feelings of guilt that I was a coward.

Eight years passed as though in an instant.

I am writing the story of my life from the comfort of my tiny, but cozy Ikea-furnished ninth floor rental apartment near Edmonton's Legislature. Finally, at the age of 36, I have my own queen bed and can afford gear for my new hobby – snowboarding. It has been a month since I started a new job as a family school liaison coordinator. When I was twenty, I thought that at 36 I would have a successful career, a family and kids and my own home. Life, however, kept taking me back to the starting line.

In Canada it took me a few years to get a study permit to study community social work. But a year-long job hunt only resulted in lowered self-esteem and depression. I was offered a part-time job as a research assistant at the Faculty of Social Work, but this wasn't helpful in applying for permanent residency in Canada. At the same time, I was putting together my parents' refugee case and taking care of all their affairs.

The first full-time job I was offered was as an intake worker at a homeless shelter in Edmonton, which meant starting over again in a new city. Working in the homeless shelter was tough physically and emotionally. But it was also a humbling experience that made me grateful for bread and shelter and that my refugee trauma was not so debilitating that it destroyed my cognitive and physical functioning.

Most of my co-workers were immigrants like me. They came here for a better future for their children in a democratic country. However, the price was to be stripped of their former social status, education, and work experience. Old and young, everyone starts from zero at a low paid, high-risk job. Daily racist slurs were also part of the job for employees of color.

In the shelter, I could sense the loneliness of many of our clients, who very often lived without a simple hug for months. I believe that I would have suffered from post-traumatic stress disorder if I did not reach out to the Ukrainian community in Calgary. For the first year after fleeing from home I thought I would never be able to laugh from my heart again. Luckily, I joined the Ukrainian Youth Association where I found genuine understanding and emotional support. I helped with children's activities, sang songs, made my first pysanka, and volunteered to help displaced children and maimed veterans in Ukraine. All this gave meaning to my life again and helped me to feel useful and worthy. This also helped me to rediscover my own cultural roots and to better understand who I am.

You see, I was not born in Crimea. Crimea is the native land of the Crimean Tatars. When I was two, my family moved there from a small Ukrainian-speaking village in Russia close to Ukraine's eastern border. There are many such villages in that region, where Ukrainian songs and culture were preserved, but "Russian" ethnicity was stated on birth certificates. Soviet colonization did its job well – villagers were taught twisted history and forgot who they really were. Until I started asking questions at the age of 20, I did not know that all my family, except for my paternal grandfather, were ethnic Ukrainians.

The USSR collapsed when I went to school, but its rudiments remained. For example, spanking was part of discipline both at home and in the kindergarten. I will never forget how terrified I was while waiting in line to be spanked by the caregiver. I was five years old. As Viktor Frankl said, in his book *Man's Search for Meaning*, "It is not the physical pain which hurts the most (and this applies to adults as much as to punished children); it is the mental agony caused by the injustice, the unreasonableness of it all."

Both in school and other institutions (with some rare exceptions, of course) it felt like the main goal was to make you feel like you matter less than a grain of sand. I am surprised that after being called dumb sheep at school, seeing how grades were bought with gifts in the institute, and remembering mom's teachings that a woman's place is in the kitchen, I dared to apply for a Fulbright scholarship to study in the U.S.

Two years later, there I was, walking across the green lawn of an American university hugging books, just like a Beverly Hills TV show. Western professors were respectful, listened to students and, to my amazement, were even evaluated by students at the end of the year. Studying in the U.S. was the first time I ever felt that I was worth something, that I mattered and that my voice mattered.

Now, eight years later, the war in Ukraine continues and my anger continues with it. Russia's full-scale invasion is hovering above Ukraine and my best friend in Kyiv, with her one-year-old baby, started looking for the nearest bomb shelter and preparing for the worst. It is exhausting to continuously be alert, angry, and publicly active. But if not us, then who?

I hope that one day I will start painting just for fun and not only for self-care between demonstrations and fundraising for Ukraine; that I will create my new cozy home, the safest place in the world, and that I will return to the free Crimea to collect the family albums that did not fit into my two suitcases. I still don't know whether our destiny is already written or whether it's a matter of choice or a chance, but out of the blue I met the love of my life at a Ukrainian dance school after I randomly walked into a Ukrainian cultural center in Edmonton last year.

"We create from what we lack and from what we can imagine," said Fowles. In the end, the most important things in life are not things.

This story was written on February 22, 2022, a day before Russia's missiles hit several Ukrainian cities and towns, starting a full-scale war against Ukraine. A month later there were several million displaced people, hundreds of murdered civilians including children, and women and girls raped and killed in the besieged cities.

6

THE SEEMINGLY IMPOSSIBLE QUEST AND LONGING FOR CHANGE

ANUSHA KASSAN

In many ways, I am the "typical" child of an immigrant. My paternal grandparents emigrated from India to South Africa, where they raised a family of five children with very limited means during a time of great racial segregation. In the late 1960s, my father and his two sisters resettled in Canada one-by-one. My father was the only one in his family to marry someone from a different culture: my mother, a French-Canadian white woman. In this way, I grew up in a biracial, bilingual, bi-religious home, and aside from my two younger sisters, I cannot think of anyone else with a shared, intersectional, lived experience. This clash in culture was certainly present throughout my upbringing, but at the same time, it opened the door to multiple, unique opportunities to see the world in rich ways. For example, I have always felt a natural ability to empathize with the range of immigrant experiences.

Like many immigrants, my father worked six days a week, building his own business. My mother raised the children while also working full-time as a nurse. As the eldest sibling, I quickly took on a caretaking role. I modelled

25

my behaviors after my mother, who spent her career taking care of others. Aside from a few rebellious moments during my teenage years, I did everything that was expected of me. I graduated high school with an international diploma, pursued undergraduate and graduate studies in psychology, and established a successful career for myself as a psychologist and university professor. While I was tackling all these professional accomplishments, I was also falling deeply in love. My husband and I are both children of immigrants, and we naturally connected over our shared values of hard work, collectivism, and giving back. We had two elegant weddings (one Italian/Catholic and one Indian/Hindu, of course!) and eventually two beautiful children (Jasmin and Bharat). We have been privileged that my career has allowed us to leave our hometown of Montréal to live in California, Vancouver, and now Calgary.

Clearly, the sacrifices my parents made "paid off" in the sense that I was able to engage in higher education and pursue a meaningful career. I did so by successfully navigating my home culture as well as multiple Canadian systems throughout my schooling and emerging career. Because of my experiences straddling multiple systems and cultures, I have dedicated my scholarship and activism to the study of immigration, diversity, and social justice within the field of psychology.

To me, this career pursuit was the ultimate way of giving back. Through psychological research, my goal was (and still is) to expand current understandings of immigration and enrich the experiences of future generations of newcomers as they integrate into Canadian society. In parallel, it has been important for me to help train the next generation of psychologists to integrate more cultural humility into their practice. In my part time clinical work, I see almost exclusively women of color, first- and second-generation immigrants, individuals from the 2SLGBTQIA+ community, and other minoritized groups. These clients have shared endless stories about their negative experiences with psychologists who clearly did not hold adequate competency to work with diverse individuals. As such, I have worked exceptionally hard to advance a social justice framework in psychology and help establish a more inclusive, truly welcoming society in Canada. I have spent countless hours engaged in this work, sometimes to the detriment of spending quality time with my family. Admittedly, my career has become all consuming.

What I recognize now, more than 10 years after graduating, is that sadly, the systemic changes needed to help immigrant communities are extremely challenging to implement. This profound realization has led me to question my personal identities and upbringing. I have been reflecting on the values that have been instilled in me, and many other children of immigrants, wondering why we did not talk about the role of colonialism and capitalism in our household. I do not think that my parents ever questioned the hopes and expectations they had for me and my sisters. Neither did I, for a long time.

Over the past couple of years, the COVID-19 pandemic has created a great deal of psychological uncertainty. In addition, numerous socio-political movements and conversations have resurged, centering on the rights and needs of Indigenous and Black individuals as well as other people of color. This level of attention has undoubtedly been necessary and has brought increased attention to my scholarship. At the same time, these critical shifts have led me to confront my privilege in very different ways and question the premise under which I have been operating. I realize that as an immigrant, the messages I have internalized, directly and indirectly are the need to honor my parents' sacrifices, be professionally successful, and offer my children a better life. However, many of the steps I have taken to achieve these goals have been colonial in nature and stemmed from the same values and approaches that have oppressed those with limited access, means, and privilege in Canadian society.

So, I find myself quite torn, having benefitted from multiple systems – the same oppressive systems which have marginalized me and my family. This dissonance has me questioning many aspects of my personal and professional life, and I feel at a loss. The entire premise (or promise) of immigration is built on the belief that newcomer families and communities can build better lives in Canada. I have certainly been blessed with a better life, which includes, but is not limited to, educational and occupational opportunities that have allowed for a certain degree of financial stability. However, to take advantage of these opportunities, I have had to contribute, advertently and inadvertently, to a Canadian society that is divided in terms of access, means, and class. Throughout my career thus far, I have been under the impression that I was fighting for more equity, diversity, and inclusion in the field of psychology and our society at large. I am now realizing that those efforts have not yielded the changes that are needed to create a truly welcoming society for immigrants and other minoritized individuals.

I think I have lost my motivation to fight unjust systems that perpetually marginalize immigrants and cause them so many hardships. Intellectually, I recognize that small changes and improvements have taken place; in my heart-of-hearts, I know it is simply not enough. I find moments of solace in the fact that I can help individuals in therapy, one at a time, or small groups of people through my scholarship. However, these micro steps seem like band-aids. I have prioritized all the values instilled in me and followed all the expected steps, yet I am left feeling hopeless. Until true systemic change takes place, and racist, discriminatory, unjust structures are dismantled in our society, I know I will not be able to rest. I hope that by sharing a snapshot of my story and perspective I can help add another layer of understanding to the complex reality of immigration in Canada.

7

BE YOU, YOU CAN

BENAZIR RAHMAN

I was walking in the park at lunchtime. Warm days in Calgary winters are rare. As I watched two girls skating, I tried to recall wintertime at home.

Home? I asked myself.

Bangladesh – the place I left 18 months ago.

Thinking of the comfortable winter of Bangladesh – the aroma of molasses, freshly-baked cakes (pitha) from mom's kitchen, attending wedding festivals or planning for a new holiday destination – made me feel nostalgic. In Canada, winter is different.

I had only seen snow in movies. Experiencing it for the first time was magical: snowflakes on my face and soft white cotton balls covering the streets, roofs, and trees. However, the excitement lasted for only a brief period. The layers of clothes, chilling wind, and slushy roads soon made me wonder when it would be summer again.

A voice in the park interrupted my daydreaming. A middle-aged woman on the phone was speaking in Bengali – my language! When she finished her call, I walked over.

"I am Benazir," I said in my native language.

"My name is Sabrina," she answered, looking surprised. "I moved here from Bangladesh two months back," she went on. "I miss everything – my family, friends, workplace. It is challenging here. I don't belong. I want to go home."

It was a flashback to my own fear and uncertainty 18 months earlier. I started sharing my journey with her.

Immigration is always challenging, and COVID-19 had made it worse. Moving to Canada during a pandemic with our three-year-old daughter was the hardest decision my husband and I ever made. We landed in Calgary in July 2020, leaving everything behind – established careers, loving family, and friends, just like Sabrina. But we had chosen to start a new chapter in Canada, and there was no looking back.

I joined a training program at a settlement organization, which helped me understand Canada's unique work culture and prepared me accordingly. I met 14 other struggling immigrant women and realized I am not alone on this journey; we motivated each other. Though I received professional training, practicum, and networking opportunities, the pandemic was a curse. I had faith and finally, after receiving many rejections, I heard the words I'd been waiting for: "We would like to offer you the position."

"I landed my first job in a public university," I told Sabrina, as we stood in the wintry sunshine.

"Wow! This is so exciting," she said. "You got your job so quickly. I heard it takes many years to get a decent job."

I smiled. "Well, I believe in hard work and sincerity. There are sleepless nights and preparations behind every success."

I started working remotely. During the first week, my manager introduced me to dozens of new faces. I struggled to recall their names with correct pronunciation, departments, and roles. My manager and teammates were supportive, offering me every kind of help. However, with the unique work environment, language, workloads, understanding instructions, new colleagues, I was losing myself.

I continued with my story, telling Sabrina about the new challenges of moving on-site. It was nerve-wracking trying to remember the doors, office spaces, meeting rooms. More people, more interactions, and more anxiety. Fear of being judged, fear of rejection, and always thinking, "What I am doing here? I feel like a foreigner."

Going to the office every day was overwhelming. I avoided interactions and trying new things. I tried to present myself as a confident person, but I was suffering from imposter syndrome. I knew this feeling was temporary, and I also knew I had to rescue myself.

Integration doesn't mean changing my identity or following new rules. Integration means self-acceptance and moving ahead with differences. There is one common language worldwide based on love, respect, and empathy that everyone understands. Leaving my comfort zone, I started socializing with colleagues, making connections, listening to their stories, sharing my unique story and my culture. This created a sense of belonging. Some people were interested in my story, and others were not. I wanted to share happiness and positivity.

"My workplace has become my favorite place," I told Sabrina. "Every day I look forward to seeing those smiling faces."

As a newcomer, with a lot of self-doubt, we want someone to believe us and understand our situation. I consider myself lucky to have a wonderful bunch of colleagues who consistently support me in pursuing my dreams.

Time has flown so quickly. After nine months at my job, I have become a better version of myself. I've gone from a nervous immigrant employee to a more confident one, sharing my opinions. Through my immigration and career journey, I have met other immigrant women and professionals; everyone has played an important role in my journey.

"In this immigration journey, there will be transition times," I said to Sabrina, who was looking at me hopefully. "You will feel lost, overwhelmed, or empty. But this won't last forever."

Lunchtime was almost over, and I had to go back to work.

"If I can do it, you can do it too. Never give up hope. And don't doubt yourself. Be yourself!" I saw a glimpse of hope on Sabrina's face. "You don't have to change. We all belong here. Practice gratitude. And call me if you need anything."

Leaving the park, I reflected on my immigration, thinking of the journey ahead in my new home. I am learning the language of kindness, positivity, sympathy, and unity from Canadian culture. Canada welcomes everyone and provides opportunities to find one's own identity and freedom regardless of one's country of birth, beliefs, race, or status. I don't know when exactly this unknown Calgary became my home, but it has. The unfamiliar roads, smiling strangers, diverse culture, people, even this chilling winter has become part of my heart.

As the saying goes, home is where the heart is.

8

STILL, I FEEL

CHARLOTTE ANYANGO ONG'ANG'A

I enjoyed the feeling of warmth that enveloped me as a child. Beginning my day under the hot scorching Kisumu sun was so energizing. Growing up in Kenya, my life revolved around chores, studying, and playing. We were taught how to keep our home clean and neat and how to welcome visitors. We always made extra food in case a visitor showed up unannounced.

From a tender age, I knew how to cook ugali, prepare pumpkin leaves, tilapia and omena. For our ugali meal for the week, my sister and I air dried corn on a papyrus mat, measured it in kilograms using a gorogoro then took it to a nearby posho mill for milling. Every grain of the maize flour was extremely valuable, so we whacked the posho mill to ensure all our flour was out of the machine and in our basket.

My mom spent her Sundays washing clothes before heading to the market to haul groceries for the week. My father fished with the boys until dusk. Sunday nights were chaotic. To prepare for the start of our classes on Monday, we would organize our school bags and iron our uniforms. Education was of paramount importance. We were often reminded that education is the only path to a fulfilling life.

My mother was a teacher at my school – Mrs. Obiero, who taught mathematics and Kiswahili. She was no-nonsense! If I misbehaved, she would grip my cheeks, and pull them like a dog's leash. Anything around her was a tool for discipline – cooking sticks, slippers, even bare hands. She was, and still is, a wonderful mother. Her priority was feeding us first then scrounging for leftovers. With her meager salary of $30 a month, she made sure we were well dressed and well fed.

Playing with other children was a big part of our day. There were always children in the neighborhood to play with. We didn't care whose children they were, whether they were the cart-puller's, cobbler's, or the mayor's. All children were equal, and all parents could discipline us if they had to. We played and danced barefoot, screamed, and shouted and nothing else mattered. I still remember the warmth I felt as my feet caressed the soft rocks on the hot stony paths. How the grass brushed my ankles as I ran along the trails. How gashes of hot sweat shot from my face as I swung my waist deliriously in the open air of God's love.

We were taught the power of prayer at an early age. Our family observed the Sabbath as a time of worship and rest. On Friday evenings we sang hymns and read Bible verses. Saturdays were spent in church. In his role as a High Priest in our home, my father led by example and always prayed for us to receive God's light and share it with others.

As a young girl, I learnt to feel things intensely. When I woke up, I felt the breath of fresh morning air reflecting the fresh opportunities that life gives each new day. I felt the fragrant smell of lemongrass tea and fresh mandazi. I felt as it got hotter in the day and louder with sounds of children playing and women squawking, the mothers of Kondele cackling noisily with their children's names. I felt the bicycles and cars screeching, the dogs barking and birds singing. I felt the sound of rain and the smell of soil, the roaring thunder then the sudden silence of the pitch-dark nights. I felt the weight of perseverance in pain and the excitement of the biblical joy that comes in the morning.

One dark night, when I was 10, I got burnt with hot water. The pain was excruciating as large blisters sagged on my chest and back. I had to endure the throbbing pain all night before seeing the doctor the next day. My skin still bears the scars that serve as a silent reminder of how much I have overcome.

I'm an adult now and I still feel things intensely. I moved to Canada in February of 2018. There was fresh snow on the ground and the air was oh, so cold. I felt the change and became excited about what lay ahead.

I am always on the move. Many times, I have gone in the wrong direction and learned a lot as a result, accumulating many scars along the way. Other times, moving in the right direction has electrified and inspired more moves. I have moved through education and personal growth. Roles and responsibilities. Countries. One of the biggest moves in my life was to Canada.

Did I encounter any stumbling blocks? Plenty! What keeps me moving forward? Perseverance. Tough times don't last, but tough people do. But it's easier said than done. It felt as though time stopped when I faced those difficult moments.

I started my first job in Canada soon after giving birth to my son via C-section. Jaundice had kept us in the hospital for nearly two weeks. Having been a stay-at-home mom for a full year, taking care of my daughter, I began an extensive job search as soon as we were discharged. I was fortunate to be invited to an interview soon after applying, and I received an offer shortly after the interview. Within a month of my cesarian surgery, I took up my new role. Those were some of the toughest weeks of my life.

The first day of my new job, still bleeding from my infected cesarian wound, I felt a river of milk gushing from my breasts. The guilt I felt as a mother was debilitating. My heart went out to my newborn at home without me. But I needed the resources to provide my children with the best possible life.

Since immigrating to Canada, I have had many wonderful opportunities. But it has not all been smooth sailing, particularly since a few people I hold dear are very far away. Canada has offered me a favorable environment to thrive and grow as a career development specialist. Nothing beats the satisfaction of hearing that a client has been hired. Understanding the Canadian work culture has been an integral part of my job. I feel confident in my ability to help job seekers find their dream jobs. As I move through life, I feel gratitude to those who have held my hand.

During the summer months, I feel the heat of the Calgarian summer and enjoy the refreshing, cool Rocky Mountain breeze. In winter, I feel the freshness of snow on the ground and the air oh so cold. Canada is my other home and, just like Kenya, I adore this beautiful country!

As I write this story, my house is a chaotic jumble. There is a pile of laundry, and what feels like a million other things demanding my attention. But I choose to feel at ease. I choose to feel relaxed. Watching my children play so innocently with so much energy, I know someday they will feel the strain of worldly responsibilities. My goal is to teach them that no matter what pressures pull them in different directions, it's okay to take a moment and feel.

9

PAST, PRESENT, FUTURE (OR THAT TIME I WROTE ABOUT MYSELF IN 1500 WORDS OR LESS)

CHELSEA YANG-SMITH

PAST
(or that time my mom bribed me with
Pokémon cards so I would learn English)

When I was younger, I remember many evenings sitting at the dining room table beside my mom, staring at a kid's activity textbook for ages 5-8, with English and grammar comprehension exercises. Mom gave me a reward – some might call it a bribe – for each lesson I completed. A full box of Pokémon cards sat on the opposite end of the table, just out of reach.

Despite English being my mom's second language, she sat with me through every lesson and helped each time I struggled. She would then hand me a pack of Pokémon cards and watch me unwrap my bribe with glee.

I never questioned those additional prep lessons. My young brain liked reading, and this seemed a fair trade for

Pokémon cards. Once I started attending elementary school, the curriculum included an advanced program for English phonograms and reading and writing comprehension. To my mother's relief and delight, I excelled in language arts and had no trouble keeping up with the class.

In grade 4, I begged my mom to enroll me in Chinese school. My school friends often spoke Cantonese and despite having an Asian last name, I was embarrassed that I couldn't speak any language other than English. I wanted to speak Cantonese with my friends. I wanted to fit in. Chinese school was going to grant me access to this secret language!

It didn't take long for Chinese school weekends to develop into a source of anxiety as I struggled to keep up with the other students. Neither of my parents spoke Mandarin or Cantonese and I didn't have the advantage of being able to practice at home. I was a terrible student. I was last in class, and because I was biracial, I looked different to my peers. I felt very isolated and alienated. It was clear that I didn't fit in here.

• • • ●•● • • •

PRESENT
(or that time I went to art school for five years
and all I got was a very expensive piece of paper)

In art school, I felt for the first time as though I truly belonged. I was weird. My classmates were weird. My instructors were weird. We celebrated our collective weirdness together. (Did you even go to art school if you *didn't* get a shitty stick n' poke tattoo in somebody's drawing studio after hours?)

In addition to my studio classes, I was required to take courses in English, humanities, and art history. Many of these classes involved reading and essay writing, a skill I was lucky to be fluent in. Artist statements, bios, grant applications, project proposals, and cover letters were all part of being an artist (and your grade) and required proficiency in English.

It didn't occur to me then that the education and extra hours my mother invested in me (only to deliver the bad news that I wanted to be an artist, not a doctor as she'd hoped) was not something every student had access to.

This only became apparent later, during critiques, where I observed instructors put students down because English was their second language. The pale saturation of my skin and fluency in English had successfully assimilated me — just as my mother had hoped.

I did well in my studies, finished my degree, and found work in my industry. I was able to engage in hyper-academic spaces. I spoke English, had a firm grasp of the esoteric art lingo, and was accepted for exhibitions, residencies, and grants. I did everything right. But I was still passed over for a highly sought-after position at the university, in favor of a white, male candidate.

This was one of the biggest letdowns I've ever experienced in my life. I was informed that we were equally matched in skills and qualifications, but it had come down to 'personality fit.' I felt betrayed and angry. I thought art school was a safe space and that I belonged (as long as I was able to assimilate properly). I can't change that I was assigned female at birth or that I'm mixed race. I speak English 'well' and I had enough experience to get my foot in the door, but I wasn't who they were looking for—whatever that means. I don't fit in here either.

● ● ● ● ● ● ● ● ● ●

FUTURE
(or that time where I don't feel confused when I look in a mirror and see myself)

Growing up in Canada as a second-generation immigrant, these are the things I know to be true: my mother immigrated from Yangon, Myanmar when she was a young teen; I have never met my cousins, aunts, and relatives currently residing in Burma; as I write this Myanmar is still under a civil war after a military coup.

I cannot even begin to understand the sacrifices my grandfather and grandmother made to bring my mother and her siblings to Canada. These sacrifices influenced my upbringing, and directly contributed to the invisible advantage of being a fluent English-speaking Canadian citizen.

I don't have any ties to the Burmese language because I never learned to speak it at home, since my mother prioritized English. I explain to strangers that I'm half Asian, half Caucasian, because it's easier than trying to point out Myanmar on a map or share any personal knowledge I have on the country outside of what you can look up on Wikipedia.

The closest I've come to embracing my Burmese heritage has been through my own self-guided research and experimentation in the kitchen. I've just started learning how to cook Burmese dishes such as mohinga (fish soup) and lahpet thoke (tea salad). I'm slowly coming around to identifying as Burmese Canadian. I check the box for Southeastern Asia when surveys ask. I badger my mother and grandmother frequently to share stories of Burma. I get political books about Aung San Suu Kyi from the library. I look up new recipes to try at home – even though I have no idea what it'll taste like or if I made it right.

I hope that one day I can visit my mother's place of birth. I hope that one day I can feel wholly comfortable in my mixed identity and find a place where I fit in. I hope that one day I can confidently say, "Hi, my name is Chelsea, and I am proudly Burmese Canadian and honor the legacy that lives on within me."

10

⸺ ◆ ⸺

NOT HERE, NOR THERE

CYNTHIA CABRERA

Dear Mom,
   Six hundred and seven days have passed and there is not a word. I had told my boss I needed a job only for a few months. That this was only temporary. I don't know what to say anymore. Every day seems the same while waiting.

Six hundred and seven days have passed. I didn't want a better job. I didn't want to make new friends or start anything I might leave interrupted. I didn't want to buy new things I might need to leave behind. I didn't want to grow my roots any deeper. But as the months turn to years, the world I have built for myself inside my head starts to crumble. Everyone around me has questions. It has been so long since I started announcing that I'm leaving that everyone wonders what went wrong.

I can't stand the questions anymore. I just want to hide. I'm embarrassed and afraid that he and I will never be together. I don't even remember what my husband looks like. The image on the screen barely resembles the kind person I fell in love with. I miss his arms, the scent of his neck, the warmth of his chest. What if we have grown apart? What if we don't like each other anymore?

45

Maybe it's time to create something meaningful with the time I have left here. This gap in time might be my chance to do what I always wanted to do – paint. I will find refuge on the canvas, new friends in the paintbrush and the pigment.

Do you remember telling me that it was the most important job that ever was? Doctors heal our bodies, you said, but art can heal our minds. It reminds us of why it's worth being alive and makes us ask the bigger questions.

I just did it, Mom! I signed up for art classes. Yes! I'm smiling for the first time in months. Somehow the prospect of a new day seems appealing again. I will have something to share when people ask. Maybe it's not so bad. I get to spend more time with you. With my brother gone, I enjoy your company more. I like you and my life here. I'm not desperate to leave, but when I do, your life will be much easier. It will take a bit, but we'll catch up, pay our debt, and start getting ahead. Then we will fix the house and buy you a piano. You will have no more need, you'll see.

I'm sorry you must get by with so little, if there isn't much for us, you have even less. My heart cringes at the memory of you crying over your ripped shoes. That face you make when there isn't more at the table and we complain; the time you had to go to that wedding in my aunt's old dress.

Six hundred and eight days have passed. I receive the call. So long I've waited without a word. I'm sobbing so uncontrollably I can't hear my own voice. They sent an email, if I'm still interested.

I gather all my fears and set out to take care of the last few steps. You, my brother, and my dad lift me up when I have no strength left. You are always here for me. I owe you everything. Thank you for accompanying me to the capital to get those papers. I had you right in front of me all this time, but I didn't appreciate you. I was so caught up thinking of tomorrow that I missed today. You were dying but I didn't know. I just wanted to be somewhere else, to start living.

I'm sorry.

This is the story of how I came to be. The story of who I left on the other side. The story of the ones that hold me here. The life I vacated.

Now I am not here nor there. One hundred and twenty-one days have passed since I arrived. Reunited with my husband at last, was in many ways like meeting him for the first time. There was joy and nervous laughter, a thousand dreams scrambled in one awkward kiss. Life was good. From the first suffocating days, my first interviews and landing a job, smiling every day when I woke up. But today, I do not smile. Because today I found out you are dying Mom. That cough that you had was not an allergy. Those weird symptoms were not stress related. You don't have much time left. How can I be far away? How can I enjoy anything I have? I never made your life better. I ran out of time.

The most difficult part of living on the other side will always be the nagging feeling of missing out. Family and friends continue to grow and change and love without you. You are removed from the everyday joys of family reunions, weddings, and new babies. But even worse is missing the funerals of the people you love most.

I'm sorry I wasn't there to lay you to rest, Mom. I knew you were leaving when I said goodbye. I wanted to hold your hand at the end, to close your eyes and kiss you. Now I get to spread your ashes to the wind. I let you go for your last flight, with nothing to hold, a bitter goodbye.

Two thousand, five hundred and fifty-five days have passed, and the shadow of your presence still haunts me. I long for the place that holds your memories, the rest of the life you lost. "Mi querido viejo" that won't ever visit. The people that own the smiles you gave them. The songs that carry your voice and the faith that parted with you. I went back but I don't know if you were there. The family that we once were lays down to rest with you.

Sometimes I imagine you are still on the other side of the phone. I feel you in the hugs of my children, in my brother's demeanor, in my father's essence, in my singing voice. I talk to the wind to say I'm sorry.

Now back home in Canada I take my brush and paint. Thank you for that. Thank you for hope, for reminding me to make it count. That it doesn't matter where I am, or who I'm with, I'm always going to miss someone.

I repeat myself over again like chanting: Enjoy where you are. Love who you are with. The most important person is the one in front of you.

Love you always,
Cynthia

11

THE MAGIC OF KINDNESS

ELENA ESINA

Thirteen years ago, I was exploring the streets of Calgary, trying to imagine my new life there. I gazed at downtown skyscrapers, counting the financial headquarters, because that's where I was planning to work – on the fiftieth floor of one of those buildings. I checked the length of the bike paths, picturing myself on a bicycle, with a trailer for my toddler. I looked at the houses, seeing us living in one with a backyard. Oh, was I dreaming!

I was half a world away from Calgary, at my computer in Russia, using Google's new Street View feature. It was pure magic – exploring the streets of a faraway city that would become my family's new home.

My dreams were big, but little did I know what that truly meant. It was only when I saw my "Welcome to Canada" visa in my passport, that I realized that there was no destination city designated – only the country. I called the Canadian embassy to ask whether we would be required to live in a particular city. To my surprise, we could go anywhere! After living my entire life in a country with a system of residency permits limiting even internal migration to the nearest town, I was overwhelmed with the realization that I had a choice now – a choice of where to live and a right to move freely anywhere I desired.

As I walked through the streets of Petrozavodsk, my hometown in Russia, my smile glowed brighter than the sunrise, making everyone around me uncomfortable. (Smiling at strangers is not a cultural norm in Russia.) Nobody knew about our plans to move yet, but here I was, on cloud nine, looking for the best place to settle in Canada.

I was 27 years old when we landed in Calgary – a city we had never been to before. Although we had done our newcomer homework very diligently, moving with a two-year-old, limited cash, no relatives, and our entire life in a few suitcases, meant that we would need to act fast. The thrill of adrenaline mixed with anxiety, helped. But what we had to learn – quickly – was how to trust strangers and let them help us.

As we passed through the final gate at Calgary International, we saw a couple holding a photo of our family of three. It was the photo I had sent to a young woman, Lindsay, whom I had met online. She was part of a travel platform I had joined, to learn more about our new destination – her hometown.

Lindsay had noticed that we were born on the same day, month, and year. We joked about the coincidence: two girls born at the same time in different parts of the world. When she asked about our arrival date and offered to help, I did not think much about it because, truthfully, our birth date was the only connection between us. Over time though, it became clear that she meant to follow through. Even though Lindsay did not live in Calgary at that time, her parents and grandparents did, and she arranged for them to meet us when we landed in Canada.

Walking towards Lindsay's grandparents at the airport was not just one of those highs where you need to remember to breathe; it was a leap from one life to another. From a life with a full-time job, an apartment, friends, and relatives, to a life that needed to be built from scratch. It was like stepping off a cliff, hoping for a stranger to catch not just you, but your whole family.

Genie and Helmut greeted us with a smile, drove us to their house, and let us stay in their three-bedroom basement suite with a stocked fridge, toys for our son, and a *Welcome to Canada* postcard in the living room. The following day, Lindsay's parents, Caroll and Doug, arrived, ready to help.

Being first- and second-generation immigrants themselves, they understood what it takes. They asked about our journey, and offered help, knowing that professional immigrants are a central pillar of Canada's economy. Asking for nothing in return, they made us feel as though we belonged – the most precious gift for a newcomer. Instead of asking why we had come, they embraced our arrival. Instead of commenting on our accents, they helped us finish our sentences and made us laugh. Instead of reminding us that we were on our own, they introduced us to their family and networks and drove us to banks, doctors, and interviews.

We did not just learn how to trust strangers; we became part of a family that had been in Canada for three generations. They were there for us each step of the way, supporting, guiding, and empowering us. My birthday sister became my soul sister, and we joined forces. It was like receiving a bigger, better parachute to help us enjoy that thrilling leap of faith into our new life.

And it was just the beginning. Kindness and compassion kept coming our way. I am forever grateful to the

Russian-speaking immigrant community for all the conversations, suggestions, and support; to all the professionals, mentors, and instructors I met on this journey before, during, and after immigration; to the bus drivers, bank tellers, receptionists, and all types of representatives on the other side of the phone who showed compassion; to all the immigrant-serving agencies, especially Calgary Immigrant Women's Association, that provided the much-desired first Canadian work experience and opened the door to the labour market; and, of course, to the employers, colleagues, and new friends who gave me a chance. The muscles in my face had begun to hurt, not from curling my tongue around a new language but from the smile that had become a fixture on my face.

Prior to boarding that life-changing flight from Russia, my family had met all the requirements under the Federal Skilled Worker Program and was granted permanent residence as professional immigrants. One memorable aspect of that process was that I became the primary applicant on our immigration application, which meant that it was up to me to score most of the required points. I got points for my age, education, relevant work experience, and level of English (in writing, reading, speaking, and listening).

The whole family had to undergo medical tests and criminal checks to confirm that we were healthy and did not pose any danger. Finally, there were adaptability points. It was like getting a GPA (Grade Point Average) at the end of high school, but the expanded version that goes beyond professional skills and experience for the entire family. If you pass, you are "good enough" to be welcomed into Canada and then it is up to you to prove in practice that you can become a successful contributing citizen in a new country.

So, getting that approval was not just a green light to travel but a message saying that Canada needed and welcomed us.

We received our Canadian permanent residency status at the airport upon our arrival, and five long years later, we became Canadian citizens. This one sentence is deceptively simple because the roller coaster immigration journey is anything but simple. There were moments when the emotional valleys were so deep that I was unsure how to climb out, and the highs happened at such an accelerated pace that I had to remind myself to breathe. The roller coaster immigration ride took me to my deepest fears and insecurities and challenged me daily to step outside my comfort zone. Getting off the ride didn't seem possible. Even when it stopped, I felt dizzy, and then hung on as it started back up again. Over. And over. And over.

Despite all the challenges, I was lucky to experience the heart of it – the kindness of strangers who welcomed me and my family and showed that they cared. Because of those strangers, I've been giving back to the community ever since that first smile at the gate.

We notice, we remember, and we are truly grateful. Many thanks to all of you.

12

IN MY OWN WORDS

EMILY YU

My memories of kindergarten are like videos on mute. The images are vivid: Easter egg hunts, Lite Brite, and a friend with whom I would exchange handmade necklaces. I only spoke Cantonese back then, so the English words that swirled around me in that classroom never settled in my mind.

I wonder if my dad's first memories of Canada are also on mute. He arrived at Edmonton International Airport with forged papers and hopes of escaping the shambles of his life in Hong Kong. He found himself unable to leave the airport because he had nowhere to go and no English words to use for help. By a stroke of luck, he met a kind stranger who also spoke Cantonese, a rarity in the 1970s, and he offered my dad a place to stay so he could get his bearings.

He found work in a shady downtown bar, and his co-worker taught him English between shifts. Tirelessly, he traced the English alphabet over and over again, eventually managing to write, but only in capital letters. I used to think that it was funny that he couldn't write in lower-case; now I know it is a skill that I took for granted.

When one of his coworkers said, "Hey buddy!", the word *buddy* was one that didn't register in his limited vocabulary, and he worried that it was something offensive, like *bloody*. He flashed back to the times new words were thrown at him that turned out to be racial slurs, so he thought it would be safer to err on the side of an insult, and he punched the guy in the face.

When I was four years old, new neighbors with young daughters moved in across the street. The eldest, Amanda, was the same age as me. The first time I visited her house, Amanda showed me her toys. One of them was a Little Tikes tricycle, still in the box. She pointed to the icon in the corner indicating the age requirements to safely play with it.

"This means you have to be two years or older," she said. "Are you more than two years old?"

I didn't know how to say my age in English, and I couldn't remember what number the English word *two* translated to. I shook my head, just in case I wasn't old enough, and I cast a last glance at the tricycle as we moved on to a different toy.

I went home that afternoon and asked my grandparents in Cantonese, "What's *four* in English?"

Even my grandparents, who only knew a handful of English words, were able to give me the right answer, and I felt like such a fool. I was proudly four years old, a fact I could not convey to a new friend, leading her to believe that I was a baby.

My mom went to an English school in Hong Kong, so she came to Canada for high school already knowing the language. When she arrived, she didn't know that her English wasn't the same as Canadian English. There were sounds that her mouth couldn't form: the letter *r* would sound like *w*, and the *k* in words like *like* would disappear.

Her speech was discordant and choppy instead of melodious. Although she never let this stop her in her endeavors, it was always in the back of her mind.

She would ask me about pronunciation of unfamiliar words and sounds that her mouth couldn't form; these things reminded her that she was different from her coworkers.

She emphasized that it was vital that I master the English language, and she made sure of this by having me read every night before bed. My room was littered with children's magazines and chapter books from the local library. When my school offered the Scholastic Book Fair, my mom would circle different items for pre-order. I always wondered how she chose which ones to buy because she didn't always ask me. Perhaps they were the books that she would have wanted to read when she was a kid. I never complained, grateful to have books to call my own, ones that whisked me away to other worlds, ones that showed me experiences that I'd never come across, and ones that gave names to emotions that I'd only known by feeling. As I grew up and tried to find my place in the world, the stories empowered me, reminding me that anyone could be anybody, and I could be my own hero. I fell so in love with stories that I wanted to create them. I wanted to tell stories that weren't being told, or rather the stories that others may not have had the words to tell.

When I started writing in high school, I thought that if I ever published a novel, I'd have to hide behind a penname. Back then, authors with names like mine didn't have books featured at the mainstream bookstore. My English first name could stay, but I'd have to choose a different last name and I hated that idea. My dad chose the name *Emily* for how it sounded combined with my last name *Yu*. *Emily Yu*. It was a name that he could pronounce, a name that rolled off the tongue beautifully, my dad's first and only English poem. My name was representative of me: half Chinese, half Canadian. To blaze a different last name across a book cover felt like a betrayal of him and of myself, especially if the sole purpose was to hide my Chinese identity.

My writing alias was not a thought that occupied me for very long though as I knew I would have to focus on getting a job that was approved by my Chinese mom. No matter how much my heart longed for it, anything related to the arts was not deemed financially stable enough. My parents endured the hardship of living with little: eating dollar-store sardines with plain rice because that was all they could afford, sitting on the living room floor because furniture was too expensive, and sleeping in fragments between deliveries because working multiple jobs meant that not a single minute could be wasted – they would not have me live the same way. I buried my dreams until they resurfaced on their own.

While working my Chinese mother-approved job, the yearning to create stories grew within me until I started to write once again. By now, names in every language adorned the covers of the bestsellers lists. All at once, I was grateful that I'd no longer have to hide my Chinese name and ashamed that I wasn't one of the pioneers who proudly flaunted their blatantly non-English names on those books.

My first published story was a fictional tale about a young woman born in Canada to Chinese immigrants and her struggle straddling her two worlds of cultural identity. I didn't realize that people would be interested in reading about this reflection of my own struggle: trying to appear more Canadian but always afraid of losing my Chinese roots, living life in the in-between. I didn't anticipate that other people would relate to my story, sending me messages of how much it spoke to them. I didn't know that my mom would ask to read my story when I told her about it, because she'd never read anything that I'd written in my entire life. I didn't expect these things to fill a hole in me that I didn't know I had.

Never again would English make a fool out of me, not like all those years ago with my neighborhood friend. Now as I keep on writing, I wield language as a tool to forge my own stories, these words that once weighed us down – now they lift me up.

13

JASMINE FLOWERS

GAYATHRI SHUKLA

E ven now, the fragrance of jasmine flowers transports me
to carefree childhood vacations with my grandparents
in southern India, where it's customary for girls and women
to wear jasmine flowers in their hair.

Street vendors sold us the flowers outside our front
porch, where my grandmother, Patti, would draw a Kolam
every morning. Kolam, made of ground rice flour, gave the
home's entrance a decorative appeal and nourished pecking
birds and ants. After assisting Patti with the Kolam, I would
head inside. Past the wooden swing in the living room. Past
the mortar-and-pestle in the kitchen used to grind dosa
batter (a rice-based delicacy). Past the aromatic sandalwood
station. Past the bucket-and-pulley groundwater well in
the backyard. Up to the terrace. I would spend many hot
summer days there, overlooking the lush green landscape
dotted with coconut trees and maroon tiled-slate rooftops,
with the Bay of Bengal stretching beyond.

Later in the day, I would take beach strolls with my
grandfather, Thatha, where we snacked on salty roasted
peanuts served in a paper cone. During these strolls, I came
face-to-face with the inequities around us. It didn't seem

fair in my young mind that the question of whether or not one could afford basic life necessities was pre-determined by birth.

When we got home, Patti would braid my hair and affix the jasmine flowers. And she would tell me stories of struggles and heartaches, of unfulfilled dreams and unparalleled triumphs.

I learned much about my grandmothers' lives through their stories. Both came of age in the 1940s when India had just crossed the bridge to independence from British colonial rule. In those days, girls were not allowed to extend their education beyond middle school, learn English, or pursue careers. They were typically married by their teenage years. Large families were common, and unsurprisingly, women championed the lion's share of childrearing.

On my paternal side, Patti raised seven children. She told me about her unassisted homebirths and even some miscarriages. She described their humble beginnings and how they saved up money for all seven children to receive a college education. She beamed with pride when she talked about her firstborn, my dad. He was the first to earn an engineering degree and work abroad at a refinery in Saudi Arabia (which is where I lived from age three).

From Patti, I learned that education was a deeply held family value and a gateway towards financial sustenance. I also discovered that she had picked my name at birth: Gayathri is a powerful mantra that invokes the life-giving force of the universe.

After the summer vacation, we would return to Saudi, exchanging lush tropics and coconut trees for sandy deserts and palm trees. Life in Saudi was comfortable for an ex-pat family, affording my brother and myself access to private schools. Yet, as I started to grow up, I felt the pangs of being the 'other.' I didn't speak the local language, Arabic, or belong to the majority faith, Islam. Being a female also meant that I was excluded from pursuing higher education after grade 10, and from entering most career fields. At the time, women were also not allowed to drive.

While these factors prompted my parents to rethink our future in the Kingdom, the tipping point was the Gulf War. We were relatively removed in our town of Al-Jubail, but we prepared for the worst. When emergency sirens punctuated the air, we donned gas masks and crouched under desks to practice bracing for an explosion. Once, a beach stroll turned a cherished family pastime into a horrific experience, as we witnessed the remnants of oil-coated ducks washing up on the Persian Gulf shore in the aftermath of the war's 1991 oil spill. It instilled in my young heart a deep desire for peace and belonging.

My family immigrated to Canada when I was 15 years old. Our plane touched down in Calgary, Alberta, on a clear August afternoon in 1998. Just like that, we traded warm beaches for the majestic Rockies, coconut and palm trees for evergreen pine, and just about everything else we knew, for the unknown. Although it wasn't our first time adapting to a new culture, the rules had changed. In Saudi, ex-pats were segregated from locals, but in Canada the goal was integration.

My brother and I swiftly adapted our English to mirror the Canadian accent. We replaced words in our vocabulary like "queue" and "rubber" with "line-up" and "eraser." We added winter jackets to our wardrobe and packed away our traditional wear. I stopped braiding my hair, and the scent of jasmine flowers faded to a distant memory. But that was only the tip of the iceberg.

Deeper struggles ensued as my dad could not find employment in his field. He was repeatedly told that he lacked Canadian work experience. Ironically, his engineering experience, as a skilled worker, had enabled our immigration. He returned to university to pursue a diploma in software technology, switching career tracks in his late 40s. My mom, with a chemistry degree, worked entry-level cashier and bank teller jobs to pay the bills.

My parents' determination to remain grounded to our roots juxtaposed our efforts to fit in. We spoke our mother tongue (Tamil) at home, retained our culinary practices (to this day, I'm a vegetarian and still relish dosas), and befriended other Indian families. Most importantly, my parents upheld the value of education. The bar of academic excellence was set high for me and my brother.

I enrolled in an advanced curriculum program in high school called International Baccalaureate. A family friend cautioned, "Immigrant? Better work twice as hard!"

Some even went a step further, advising me to consider anglicizing my ethnic-sounding name, as that would improve my chances of securing future job opportunities. I resisted of course. Patti had given me my name and that meant the universe to me.

But to work hard? I had that in spades. I earned my way into engineering through scholarships at the University of Calgary. The advice lingered. A female mentor warned, "Woman in engineering? Better work twice as hard!"

This time, I decided to work hard by learning my craft hands-on. I made the bold move to Fort McMurray by myself at the age of 20. As one of the few women of

Indian origin working in an industrial setting, I felt the pangs of being the 'other' again. But I learned to excel in the profession despite doubts that would surface about my competencies. My secret sauce, it turned out, was storytelling.

Initially, my stories were reflections I wrote to myself about my struggles and strengths. Over time, this enabled me to reclaim my authentic voice. I also realized that by sharing stories with others, I could nurture a sense of community and help others to appreciate diversity.

What I knew intuitively about the power of stories was confirmed during my MBA, an arduous endeavour undertaken while working full-time and parenting two young kids. I specialized in social impact and studied how to co-create inclusive cultures by harnessing a community's lived experiences. It helped me envision the impact I wanted my career to have – to shape a world that celebrates its diversity and shared humanity, starting with my beloved home, Canada.

I fell in love with Canada, not because my immigration experience was bereft of challenges. It wasn't an easy journey, and I am not alone in that regard. I also painfully recognize that our history holds a dark chapter of terrible harms inflicted upon Indigenous communities, the original peoples of this land. But I have experienced a side of Canada that embraces democracy, multiculturalism, and peace. This Canada welcomed me into her open arms and propelled me to soar high.

In 2007, I travelled to India for my wedding and met Patti. As she braided my hair and affixed jasmine flowers, I told her that I was following in her son's footsteps with my engineering career in Canada. I will never forget her voice brimming with joy, for this was an unimaginable feat in her day. Sadly, it was the last time we met in our ancestral town of Nagapattinam. Both my grandmothers passed away peacefully in subsequent years.

Today, I have a small jasmine plant in my home. Every time there is a new bud, I am reminded of my grandmothers' everlasting love and our unbreakable family values. In trading old for new, I wish not to forget my roots. As I continue to spread my wings, I strive to create a better future for generations to come.

14

A LOVE LETTER TO MY YOUNGER SELF

GERI LIVELL

My dear Geri,
As I write this letter to you, you are only 10 years old, on a family trip to China. For the first time, all four of you (mom, dad, big sister, and you) travelled together. On this trip, you discovered your mom's country. You don't know it yet, but you are going to have the opportunity to experience immigration, like your mom did when she left China to settle in French Polynesia, your home country. Does this surprise you? To know that you will leave French Polynesia and settle in another country?

"Isn't that what some Polynesian students do anyway?" you might ask.

And you would be right. Some leave French Polynesia to pursue their studies at universities in France, Australia, United States, and Canada. Their move is usually temporary, and they return to French Polynesia at the end of their studies.

But you will decide to create your own path, my dear Geri.

You will study in Montpellier, France, before spending 17 years of your life in Canada. You will meet friendship, kindness, and love, but also loss, sadness, and despair. Alone in your apartment, sitting at your desk, staring at a blank page, you will wonder about your life, your future. The words, *who am I?* will flash continually through your mind. You will look for signs and direction, searching for your wonderland, using a compass with no due North.

You will ask: *What do I most desire?*

I am still deciphering our destiny.

Keep this in mind, little Geri: everything happens for a reason. Every person you meet, every emotion you feel, will be exactly what you need to help you find your true self. It will take faith and courage to study, work and leave your family at age 17.

You may wonder: *How will I feel moving to Canada?*

Well, besides feeling cold, you will feel excitement, but no fear. You will discover a new life, a new culture, meet new friends. And as unlikely as it may sound, you will decide to start this new chapter for love, to feel the same chills you felt watching the adventures of Indiana Jones, but without the scorpions, mice, snakes, and bugs, thank you very much!

You may be concerned: *What will be my challenges in Canada?*

Don't worry, the challenges are opportunities for growth, for finding who you are. You will have lots of opportunities to learn, and improve, and this will bring you closer to your true self. One of your struggles will be to speak English.

Even now, at age 10, you understand what I mean. You remember the day your heart was pounding like a punching ball? When you opened your mouth to speak but all that came out was silence? Your mom's friend had asked you a simple question. She was a friendly lady, so what was the problem? She spoke the Chinese dialect you could understand but could not speak without sounding like a foreigner.

How many times did people laugh at you because of your accent? I wish I could tell you it won't happen again, but even in the future, outsiders will not see you the way you really are. You will try to be outgoing, friendly, sociable, but let's be honest: you are an introvert! And the beauty about being an introvert is that you will learn to listen to others with your heart, with kindness, and with compassion. You will understand the importance of friendship, of keeping an open heart, of being you and present in the moment. And that will be your gift – to yourself, and to your friends and family because you will give them your attention, your time, and your love.

In Calgary, you will remember your love for dance. You will always remember your first jazz dance performance as a teenager: your sweaty hands, dry lips, the stress balanced by joy, your smile before, during and after your performance.

Dancing is a conversation with your body, a shared moment with your true self. George Balanchine said, "See the music, hear the dance." Will you believe me if I tell you that you will stop dancing? I can hear you scream: *No! Why would I do such thing?*

The reasons will be both financial and personal. You won't dance for many years. But one day, walking home from work, your hands in your pockets, without warning, your love of dance will awaken your spirit. You will see an advertisement for a dance performance. You will know nothing about the school, but you will recognize the theme, the characters, the make-up, the costumes, and of course the scar on the boy's forehead. That performance will be the turning point, when your heart and soul recognize what they have been seeking.

I know it is difficult to understand. Even now I still have questions. Sometimes, we just don't know what we are supposed to be or do. But remember this: everything in life is as it should be. And once you realize that you will open your heart, be at peace with yourself and feel grateful for all your gifts.

My dear Geri, there is so much to learn in life! Follow your heart and believe in yourself.

With love,

Your forty-something older self

15

DEAR HUMI JAAN

HUMIRAH SULTANI

I have this old photo of you in my hands, a picture from when you were young. It's the only one I have of you. Even then, your smile was cautious, guarded, contained – a straight line gently inscribed across your face. The only way that I can tell that you were happy is from your eyes – bound from above by disciplined brows and overwhelmed from below by joyful cheeks. Even now, during a pandemic when we all cover our faces with masks, everyone can always tell when you're smiling. You never had time for toothy grins and silly poses, but in this photo, all the joys of your childhood are crisply preserved with a glossy finish. I know that you never liked a single picture of yourself, but I love this picture of you.

You arrived fashionably late to your best friend's birthday party – on Afghan time, as you'll come to say when you're older. I'm sure she didn't mind though as she was Afghan, too – you were blessed to find a best friend in your angelic cousin. Wearing your favorite attire, your Hazara dress and jewelry, you were ready to celebrate! You never wondered where this dress came from, yet somehow it had always been there in your life. Sometimes you did wonder though about that place that your parents called home, the one they left behind. The distance was immeasurable and the world that came to life in their stories and recollections seemed utterly unimaginable. None of your other friends could even pronounce Afghanistan, let alone understand what it meant to you. It was there that the capable hands of Hazara women crafted this dress for you. These women solved seemingly impossible problems with boundless imagination and little to no formal education. Their legacy was intricately embroidered into the yakhan, the bodice of your dress. Perhaps, by the hands of your studious mother, such delicate artisanship taught to her, handed down by her own mother. An embrace from your grandmother, one that you were never destined to feel, yet her warmth and love reached you all the same, as tightly and as snug as the bust of your dress.

Oh, how it fit you so perfectly! The vibrant jewel tones reflected the many facets of your own character. Your calf-length dress was a fiery red, burning with intense determination, strength and freewill, barely contained beneath a lattice of precise geometry. Your billowy tumban draped carelessly around your legs. It was dyed a pristine emerald green, which would forever be your favorite color. Tendrils of gold traced along every hem as though its very purpose was to tickle you with joy; laughs shared with ancestors you would never meet. Not even in black and white photographs.

You always wished that you could read a book or hear a story about a princess who looked like you. One who celebrated her femininity, beauty, and culture, all while twirling and dancing without a care – without the need for granted permissions. One who explored the world around her, challenged her oppressors and fought for freedom while running around in silky trousers and golden flats. One who would collect herbs for dawaii alaaf and prepare turmeric and egg poultices like khaambad as she learned the traditional medicines of her people. Most fairy tales would label her a witch, your favorite video game would dub her a white mage, but I was thinking more of an apothecary – a pharmacist. She could jot down notes in her pocketbook – ah, except they don't make pockets for girls anymore. Now, clothes have fake pockets embellished with gold zippers and useless details with nowhere to store important information about where we've come from and where we're going. Not that her dress or pants would have pockets either, but at least those were remnants of an age-old culture. Alas, everything that she will need to know in life would be securely archived in her mind, in that beautiful place where she will always be learning and growing.

Like when you were learning to care for your newly pierced ears, courtesy of your mother by hand and needle. You couldn't remember how much it hurt but the pain was a small price to pay. The real privilege was to make this decision all by yourself. Peeking through your hair hung ancient chandeliers, intricate silver earrings that tinkled sweetly as you would run and play. This was where your appreciation for fine details and artisanship first came to life. That's why you chose to wear this dress. It didn't matter whose birthday party it was, nor did it matter who was going to be there. You would go as yourself. Others may have laughed sheepishly by now, feeling overdressed when all the other guests were sporting t-shirts and leggings. Not you, though – you knew your outfit was perfect. There is no such thing as dressing too formally for a childhood birthday party, not when you are Afghan and especially not when you are modelling the marvelous handicraft of Hazara women.

Incredible – a woman created these clothes for you! Even more incredible – a woman created you! Of course, she could not have done it alone. Alongside your mother was an entire community of women and girls who have uplifted, empowered, and raised you. Especially your dearest aunt – yes, the one you were dying to meet. The drive to the airport to welcome her and her family to Canada was rerouted to the hospital so that your mother could give birth to you. She was your best friend's mother, your mother's best friend and sister – your aunt that cared for you like your own mother. Would that make your cousin, your best friend, your sister? Like a tangled knot, the complexity of your network of family and loved ones will forever surprise you. As you take time to unravel the strings and truly understand the immense trauma and horrors that each of these individuals faced in her own life, you will then understand the gifts she has shared with you. Through her stories, she shared her vision, insight, and empathy. Through her craft, she has gifted you with the many colors of creativity, ingenuity, and resilience. How fortunate to have inherited such wealth; lustrous threads to weave your own tapestry. Gently ripping stitch by stitch, you'll free yourself from the aggressive patterns that have been sewn into your generation by the hands of those with eternally broken hearts. It's too late for sutures now as their profound wounds have already scarred over. You will spend the rest of your life undoing the intergenerational trauma that has penetrated their lives and threatens to pierce through your own. Your time is well-spent as you work to prevent that same insidious needle from pricking into the next generation.

Ah, found her! There's the heroine of the epic story that you've always dreamed of – it's you! Even your family name dubs you a princess: Sultani, you're the daughter of a Sultan. You chose your weapon and armor well. They will empower and protect you as you venture forth in life, ready to mend broken hearts. Your fairy tale started in that moment when you chose to be yourself, to wear the artistry of your ancestors and to be captured in all your youthful glory in my favorite picture of you.

16

CURIOSITY STARTS WITH A BEER

INEZ ASHWORTH

I will begin where most of my childhood memories begin – in the pub. It's where I was born, in a town just outside Manchester, England and where I lived up until my late teens. It's where my curiosity for people began. I remember looking around at all the different cultures, backgrounds and ages and being amazed by how everyone got along and looked out for each other, well, most of the time anyway.

They were like my second family. From the age of eight we travelled to many different countries within Europe on brewery tours. I was happy, healthy, and loved being around different people. I was quite a character – a confident, mischievous child.

When I was 12, I stole my first bra. I blamed my mom –she said I didn't need one yet. Who was *she* to say I didn't have boobs? At 13, I got expelled from school for taking alcohol into my history class, but I saw it as a teachable moment. My dad was embarrassed, picking me up from school that day, but maybe not quite as embarrassed as picking me up from the police station for shoplifting a bra. He used to tell me that my older brothers were so much easier than me, but I always came from a place of making people happy even if my parents and teachers didn't see it that way.

I left school early to work in the local factory, with very little education. This was normal in my town, so I never saw it as a big deal. Realizing I needed some basic office skills, I went back to college while working full time. This is what society told me I needed to do to be "successful."

Life kicked in and all the things I was protected from as a child started to become reality, but I still remember the support from my pub community, my second family.

I was in a mentally abusive relationship for many years. The day it turned physical, I finally found the courage to leave. I remember sitting in the pub, beaten and bruised, seeing my dad cry for the first time while mumbling "It's going to be okay."

In my early twenties, several health issues began. Over the years, they progressed, but I always told myself to be grateful: so many people had it way worse than I did. In my forties, I was diagnosed with an illness that really tested my strength. Anti-depressants were prescribed, but after just a couple of months I realized they were taking away my empathy – a big part of my identity. Luckily, I found a path forward and I am now the healthiest I have ever been.

I never thought I would be in a trusting relationship again, but someone came along who encouraged me, gave me back my confidence and made me feel safe – my soulmate, and now my husband of nearly 30 years.

Immigrating to Canada seemed like an easy thing to do. But then reality hit, and I realized I would be leaving behind my friends, family, the people I had grown up with, my support system, and the traditions and norms I was used to. As a daughter, the realization that I was leaving my mum and dad struck hard. I wouldn't be able to pop in for a coffee or celebrate milestones. I wondered if I would ever see them again. If anything happened, would I make it home in time to say goodbye?

Settling in Canada, my lack of education came back to haunt me. At the time, I had over twenty years of recruitment experience, but not in Canada. Applying for a job online is like a black hole if you are not from Canada. When I finally got my first job, I realized I had been taken advantage of as an immigrant. I was paid minimum wage and told I needed a car and phone to secure the job. But I did what I had to do to stay in Canada, grateful for the job despite the miserable circumstances.

I adapted quickly and started networking, purposefully creating valuable connections. I joined the British expats network. While I didn't want to only socialize with people from back home, they did offer me a sense of belonging and the security of familiarity. With their help, opportunities came my way, and the transition was made easier.

It took two years, but I finally landed my first permanent position and started to make great friends and colleagues. For the first time, coming to Canada felt like the right decision. Canada is a beautiful place filled with so many opportunities (though I do wish things could be easier for immigrants).

It took me six years, lots of paperwork, and suspense, but I finally got my permanent residence. Being from England, I thought I needn't prepare for the English test. With a score of 50%, I just passed! My husband still jokes about it. I can't imagine how hard it must be for someone whose first language isn't English.

The next step was taking the citizenship test. The biggest learning I had about the land I now called home, was the history of Indigenous peoples. I started digging in, learning about this community. At my citizenship ceremony, the judge told me that I should start volunteering like other Canadians. Giving back to the community became a big part of my life. I have dedicated much time and effort to learning about people, their stories, and backgrounds. It reminds me of the curiosity of my childhood. My commitment to the community has given me the education I needed to become an advocate for others: the skills that have got me to where I need to be to be kind, open, compassionate, and make time for others. You don't need to go to school for that.

I recently celebrated my fiftieth birthday, and I am living my best life. I am an entrepreneur, with the best support network I could ask for. In my early twenties, I could never have imagined a life so full of happiness, success, and love. I get to focus on making the world a better place which is what I love to do.

My lack of education still crosses my mind and will always make me doubt myself, but recently my husband said to me, "You make the world better. Would you rather have more education or be who you are – a kind, compassionate, and resilient person?"

For all the immigrants out there, wherever you are on your journey, don't give up. You have already done the hardest part by leaving behind family and friends. I encourage you to create networks. Step forward with confidence and celebrate all your accomplishments, big and small.

17

Distances and Destinations: Healing in Hong Kong

Jesiebelle Salcedo

At the terminal, Mom and I huddled behind the pillar as I waited to board the plane for my month-long excursion to Asia.

"Mom, aren't you allowed closer?" I asked.

People around us were hustling and bustling to retrieve last minute snacks or sprint to their next flight. Announcements popped up every few minutes, but with Mom, time stood still as I clung to every moment that I could spend with her before my departure.

"No anak ko, (my child) I can't. Airport staff aren't allowed near the terminal. It's against the rules."

Earlier, Mom had used her assistant manager perks in one of the airport restaurants to feed me a hearty breakfast of eggs and bacon. At 23, I hadn't thought I would miss Mom, but as we chatted, the idea of leaving her surfaced as heartache. I studied her face as her soft brown eyes, behind square glasses, stared off into the distance. Her short black bob framed a face filled with wonder and worry, and her shoulders were scrunched up like a tightly closed book.

"Anak, it's okay," she said, her eyes crinkled like crescent moons to halt her tears. "This will be a good experience for you. You'll have so much fun."

I tried to fight back my own tears, but a few escaped as she locked me in her arms. My head knew I had to move forward, but my heart wasn't yet ready to leave her embrace.

Before Mom moved to Canada, she had immigrated to Hong Kong from the Philippines and worked as a nanny alongside two of her sisters, my Auntie Carmen and Auntie Agnes. In 1990, after two long years there (and completing many documents), Mom flew to Canada. Four years later, she gave birth to me, her eldest daughter.

Over the years, there were limited opportunities to visit my relatives in the Philippines. When we did visit, we took Balikbayan boxes with us – filled with goods from abroad like clothes, beauty products, and non-perishable foods. We always visited the same three locations: Ilocos Sur, Isabela and Manila. These trips were filled with food, sunshine, and relatives from my lolo and lolas (grandpa and grandmas), to cousins, uncles, and aunties. My last childhood visit was in 2007, when I was 13 years old.

Ten years later, in March 2017, we reunited with Mom's family in Hong Kong to celebrate her fiftieth birthday. Along with Auntie Carmen, and Auntie Agnes, other family members arrived – Krystelle my cousin, my mom's brother Uncle Lito, and most importantly, my lola, the matriarch of Mom's family. This was Lola's first and only time travelling outside of the Philippines.

We visited the night markets, indulged in delicacies, and wove between the mainland and city central on the MTR (Mass Transit Railway), making the best of our time in Hong

Kong. When it was time to leave, I decided this wouldn't be my final goodbye.

A few months after our family visit, I made a pit stop in Hong Kong during my Asia excursion. As I flew in from the land of the Khmer Empire, I admired the glimmering city skyline.

"This is what a second home must feel like," I thought on the bus enroute to Sheung Wan as I replayed my springtime family memories of Hong Kong.

Waiting at the bus stop in the rain were Auntie Carmen and Auntie Agnes smiling from ear-to-ear. With quick hugs, they swept me out of the storm and into their cozy apartment, filled with embraces and meryenda (snacks).

We scrolled through photos of my trip up to that point – of temples and foods. Slowly I opened up to Auntie Carmen and Auntie Agnes about what life was like growing up in Canada.

Much of my dad's family, in Canada and the Philippines, had strong opinions of Mom, judging her every move. If she didn't let me or my sister do something, she was overprotective. If she overreacted to a situation, she was crazy. If she said something they didn't like, she was a bitch or tsismosa (gossiper). Sure, they commended her culinary creations, and were thankful when she sent money back home, but these compliments never measured up to the tsunami of judgements. Their tsismis (gossip) over the years had distorted my perceptions of Mom.

With the opinions of my dad's family an ocean away, I asked, "Auntie, what was my mom like as a kid?"

I wanted to know what her life had been like before she had me. What were her dreams? Was she always the tense woman I'd known throughout my life?

My mom was a tough woman when I was growing up. She was a mixture of sunshine and sorrow, and sarcasm. Unapologetically honest, she could be blunt. She was ambitious, with big dreams for herself and eventually me.

As the eldest daughter, I was burdened with great expectations. For years I strived to embody the ideal daughter, cultivating a mixture of responsibility, success, and intelligence to obtain a degree, land a stable job, and make mountains of money. When I did not meet Mom's expectations, she was a thunderstorm. Saying sorry, wasn't in her repertoire at the time. Instead, she used food as an apology to break the silence between us. For a while, I feared and resented Mom slightly.

Waiting for Auntie Carmen and Auntie Agnes to respond to my question of what my mom had been like, felt like an eternity. My anxiety was running circles with infinite possibilities playing in my head.

Auntie Carmen started explaining: "Your mom was always helpful around the house, especially after your lolo's accident."

Lolo was paralyzed from the waist down when he fell out of a coconut tree when Mom was just eight years old. Mom had once told me that Lolo was gone for a few months in Manila due to this severe injury, leaving the responsibilities divided among herself and her siblings.

Auntie Agnes continued: "Anak, your mom always helped with the cooking. She would cook kanin (rice) and help wash the dishes. She studied so hard and was so smart. Lola always wanted what was best for her because she was her favourite."

For the rest of the night, they fed me anecdotes of Mom's childhood in the barangay (village). I felt a huge wave of relief and love for her.

For much of my adolescence, I had painted my mom as a villain. Dad's family's judgments had beaten her down. Over time, Mom built walls to protect herself and us. She pushed my sister and I to find paths of self-discovery rather than simply of survival. For years, I was blinded by illusions of an ideal mother instead of appreciating who she already was. My aunties' stories had opened doors of healing, filling my heart with love.

I thought back to my recent departure from Canada. Standing with Mom at the airport, I had been fearful. But Mom had taken a leap of faith when she hopped on the plane to Hong Kong years earlier, and I had to trust in myself in the same way.

Listening to my aunties' stories of my mom, I remembered her squeezing my hand tightly as she said, "I'll see you when you come back anak. Call me when you've landed. Ingat ka (you take care), I love you."

18

No Longer Just a Diary Entry

Karen Durham

I t is easier for me to tell other immigrants of my experience of coming to Canada than to tell those who have not immigrated, because we have shared stories of loneliness and isolation.

At age 13, I knew that I belonged somewhere and that I had a history. I was in Canada, but I was not Canadian. I did not fit the mold. I looked, spoke, and carried myself differently. I was Indian with an English name. English was my mother tongue, and I spoke it fluently, with an Indian accent.

Now, 25 years after arriving in this country, I feel Canadian, especially when I look for a Timmy's after an international flight or spit out a smooth "eh," but my accent still leaves people wondering.

I was always the girl with the accent. Classmates and coworkers apparently loved my accent for no other reason than it was different. I am still the girl with the accent. If only people knew I am a dime a dozen back "home." In my early days in Canada, only one friend asked about my cultural background. I have always appreciated her desire to know me better.

I am proud of my accent because it reminds me of what a fearless advocate I was as a kid and still am as an adult. I am a testament that identity can be both preserved and remain fluid. However, it is not a straightforward process.

When I first started school in Canada, the top two questions were where I had learned to speak English and where my accent was from – pointing out that I had one. This made me aware of the Canadian accent and of the words that seemed so overused, like "awesome" and "wicked." My 13-year-old-self found jollies in asking those who asked me about my accent, what accents they had.

I felt a wrong righted every time I put them in a position of having to define themselves by their accents. I made myself into a champion and felt my cause was altruistic, but hindsight shows me it was simply inflicting pain.

There was a family who immigrated at the same time as we did, who shared the same cultural background. I remember being livid when, after a mere two months of being in Canada, the kids' accents had morphed into a Canadian accent. They were about the same ages as me, so their choice was a very clear demonstration of the different paths one takes to belong. Those kids chose to do as the Romans did but I perceived the change in speech as a personal betrayal to the immigrant in me. Yet, maybe these kids got to stand out in a more authentic way, rather than for their accents. So perhaps what was a means of survival and a bid to belong became the foundation to be known in a true and meaningful way. Today, I have compassion for their choice.

Those many years ago it was not fashionable to be different in Canada. Being unique was not a good thing. The way I looked and spoke could not be pegged down and that made people cautious. In high school, it meant peers would not choose me for group work or to be on their teams. Rumors were spread when I got As on assignments. I ate my lunches in bathroom stalls and then found refuge in the library. Sometimes I sat with kinder classmates until it became dangerous for them to be seen with me. I was extremely lonely and embarrassed by it to boot.

However, reprieve came in the form of a youth minority program through which I made a lifelong friend who then became my other half in university. We soon grew our friend circle to include more outsiders. We informally referred to ourselves as the United Nations and were deeply proud and reveled in the closeness of our group. These friends accepted me wholly. They learned of my directness, creativity, and sense of humor. They welcomed my penchant for food and my personal style and embraced my curly hair. They knew things about me that no one else had ever been interested in before.

These friends are also immigrants and have their own uniquely painful experiences, yet they have shared only small pieces of these experiences with others. I wonder if, like myself, it was easier for them to bury solo lunch sessions in bathroom stalls, the accusation of being smelly because of different kitchen spices, or the judgment directed at them for being refugees and immigrants, taking away jobs from "real" Canadians.

I am utterly grateful to have experienced a disconnect because I now fully appreciate human connection. The loneliness I felt as a new immigrant continues to guide me positively. I empathize easily with others, make meaningful friendships, and have an open mind. At age 39, confident in my unique accent, I know that I belong here and that this is a treasured part of my history.

19

GROWING WITH GRACE

KARISHMA SUTAR

It takes rain and sun both to help the flower
grow
My immigration journey is a crockpot of
emotions, cooked meticulously and slow

So, when I start to write about this adventure
know that I had it all
Not just the "wow" moments and fun stories
but failure and heartbreak are also what I recall

A lot was at stake when we left our roots
We just had one thought – our child will relish
our struggle's fruits

When we landed, we were welcomed by
generous and genuine friends
We ate good food, visited mountains – what an
amazing time to spend

Reality hit when weekend ended,
Our friends went back to work, and we
suddenly felt stranded

First things first, we jumped in and started with
a basic set up
The list went on to buy several things and
expenses started to add up

After every dollar I spent, my mind would
immediately do conversions and calculate
The second thought would be, do I really need
this, my heart would evaluate

I must mention the generosity of the
volunteers who dropped off an entire month's
groceries!
We were so thankful for these people whose
warmth was extraordinary

Savings were getting low and finding a job took
the highest priority
Oh, you came at the wrong time, finding a job
is impossible, said the majority

We took the advice – take any job, there is
respect and dignity in whatever work you do
No work is big or small, just work hard, make
connections, and you will get through

We accepted that it would be hard getting
through winter so geared up with warm

clothing
But early sunsets, and chilly, lonely nights
brought heaviness and emptiness approaching

My husband found work first and began the
race to chase money
I felt homesick, frustrated, totally lost but had
a kid who was loving and funny

He was my saving grace, I looked at his face and
drew strength
Talking to my sisters was therapy – we spoke at
length

It felt like every door I used to knock was
already locked
An endless series of hard luck as if all ways were
blocked

Each day was different, some days I would hide
my emotions and pretend to be fine
Other days I would sob silently or bottle up my
anger and pray to God for a sign

Once I was alone at the bus stop with my kid
on an extremely frosty night
Every minute we waited felt like hours, he was
shivering in cold I had to hug him tight

What I felt that night still brings me tears –
thinking about that painful sight
My husband and I wanted to make sure we

never repeated this unfortunate plight

We tried hard to stay positive and hoped for a
miracle that would change the plot
We saw a brochure – links to success training
program – I would give this my best shot

The phone interview began, but after two
questions I was told I wouldn't fit in
My heart sank in fear, and I asked what was
missing

This program is for ladies who are under 30
years of age, said the lady with a gentle voice
Thoughts started racing – I can't miss this
opportunity, I don't have any other choice

Without counting numbers, I softly replied,
yes, I am already 30 but not yet 31
Please let me continue the interview and not
leave this conversation undone

The lady was impressed and continued the
interview, finally saying, Karishma, you nailed
it
I am looking forward to meeting you in person,
just work on your resume and send it

This one phone conversation changed the
game, and I did my victory dance
I still get nervous thinking what I would have
done if she hadn't taken a chance

So, she is my lady angel who proved that we
should believe in miracles
My program started and life got mundane
with deadlines, assignments, house chores so
typical

I dove in and gave it my all, made some
wonderful friends and completed the class
Along came another angel who gave me more
than I could have asked

She gave me my first job and guided each step
with patience and a strong belief
When I accepted my first job offer, both of us
were so relieved

In my first contract job I felt I was dumb,
realizing I need to learn so much – I am way
behind
But my third angel who was assigned to be my
buddy was extremely kind

She made everything look easy as she cared
enough to explain
If I still got it wrong, I could reach out again

The short-lived comfort of four months ended
As my contract was not extended

I managed to get another job in downtown
Excited and thrilled I started a countdown

New job, new role, new people, new fear
Something made me uneasy which wasn't very
clear

A few weeks into the new job, I was still not
trained fully
Everything I did, was wrong because I was
dealing with a bully

Toxic friends in my personal life and this bully
at work started taking a toll
My life was falling apart – I had no control

I understood the importance of family and
friends on whom you can depend
They love you for who you are, make time for
you and never pretend

There was a ray of hope when my sister came to
Canada and stayed with us
I'd found a close friend with whom I could
share my trouble and trust

We both sensed the same vibe, and our feelings
were mutual
We didn't belong here, and this needed to
change – it's not usual

I was constantly judged on what I looked like
and what I wore
Sweet words, cunning eyes, mean intentions,

I'd never encountered this before

For the first few years, I suffered in silence and
doubted everything I had done
I gave my power away which made them think
they'd won

I took a chance to sort things out and have a
fresh start
They refused to accept and said that the fault
was all on my part

It was time to sit back and re-think what was
causing me more trouble
To understand this was fake and time was right
to pop this friendship bubble

The office bully incident was reported, and I
was given the support I needed
Created a clear boundary and ensured the
behavior was not repeated

In my head, I carved a way to detach, cared less
and simply moved on
Took a new road, discovered a passion, and
found things to improve on

Sometimes you must burn the bridge
completely and habits need to be unlearned
Real friends don't hurt you, but one shouldn't
reciprocate the same hatred in return

I learnt to find happiness in my own people and
my family who are far but always there
My husband was my biggest strength, cheering
me up on bad days because he really cares

I shut my doors tight and didn't allow anyone
to peep in for a while
My circle got smaller, limited to the few who
gave me a smile

The reason this experience is worth
mentioning in my story
Is that how I changed in the process, is my true
glory

I gave up people pleasing, the need for constant
validation and my obsession to be liked by all
Instead, I faced the issues head on, stayed
authentic and real, stood strong and tall

Slowly my broken pieces started to come
together and made a beautiful masterpiece
I started doing well in all areas of my life as if I
found some master keys

Then, every door I knocked – opened and
made a way
When things change inside you, all the hurdles
go away

I slayed my goals one by one personally and
professionally

I found my own path to make this world a
better place individually

Charity begins at home and so all my care and
love are first for my family
We forgive each other, practice gratitude
together and live happily

I also have a small bunch of birds; we flock
together and share friendship goals
Each one is special as well as unique and each
fulfills different roles

I didn't mention a lot of the angels who played
an important part
All my favorite people with their extremely
generous hearts

I wish I could be somebody's angel too
And offer my help to someone, to help them
get through

My heart is full of gratitude for my amazing life
Let's embrace our imperfections, celebrate,
and thrive!

20

FINDING SUCCESS IN FAILURE

KAZLINDA KHALID

S ome people are born knowing the right answers to all the questions. Some people are lucky and are in the right place at the right time. Me? I got to where I am through hard work and perseverance. Looking back at all the steps I took when we arrived in this beautiful country, I recognize that some of my decisions led to failures. As it turned out, every failure taught me something important. I knew that if I was patient and optimistic, I would reach my destination in the end. After each wrong turn, I'd pick myself up and face the obstacle head-on with a spring in my step.

When we first landed in Calgary in the summer of 2017, we encountered our first challenge: finding a place to live. Little did we know how difficult it would be to find a place to rent as a newly landed immigrant. There was no way for a landlord to check my credit score because I didn't own a credit card. There was no way for them to call my previous landlords because how could I expect them to call people halfway across the world?

After days of hearing "no," we met someone who perhaps felt sorry for our little family and gave us a chance. Now, I'm a huge believer that all things happen for a reason, and everything did work out for us. The nearest school was a five-minute walk away. The preschool was right across the street and there was a dance studio nearby that would be perfect for my tiny ballerina.

The next challenge we faced was finding a job. I often get asked, "Why do you want to work?" If I wasn't a mother, would they ask me this question? Women all over the world work to put food on the table and pay for the roof over their heads. I am well aware of the privilege I have of not needing to work as my husband can pay for my necessities. In this new world we moved to, I wanted to live a life that I, my children, and my parents could be proud of. I yearned to go back to work so that I could do something that fulfilled my soul. I wanted to end each day knowing that I had made a difference in someone's life.

I started losing my sense of identity the day I got married. I was always introduced as F's wife. With the birth of my eldest daughter came a new name for me: A's mom. Somewhere along the way, my own identity became invisible. I knew if I didn't change something, I would forever be referred to as F's wife or A's mother.

I wanted to be known as Kazlinda. You know, Kazlinda, that hard-working woman who always has too many things on her plate but handles them without complaining. That's right, Kazlinda, the fun-loving girl who is always up for a night out with the girls. Yes, I was a wife and mother, but I was also many other things.

When I arrived in Canada, I was in my second trimester, expecting twins. I could not look for work. "No matter," I repeated to myself. I thought about what I could do to ensure that when my time came to join the workforce, I'd be ready. I realized that I had received a second chance to refine my skills and pursue my passions.

I've always loved helping people and advocating for them when their voices were not heard. That's what led me to pursue a law degree in Malaysia. Having a father in the armed forces and a husband who worked in the oil and gas industry, there were days when I'd wonder if they would come back home in one piece.

When we lived in Abu Dhabi, we saw construction workers in buses without air conditioning in 40°C heat. We read stories about delivery drivers rushing around to multiple destinations in the terrible heat. When injuries and deaths occurred, I often wondered what more could have been done to prevent these incidents.

After some reflection, I realized I was passionate about workplace health and safety. I wanted to speak up for those who couldn't speak for themselves and for their families. I signed up for an occupational health and safety certificate program at the University of Calgary.

Once I completed my fundamental certificate in occupational health and safety, I started searching for employment. No one would hire me without experience. Defeated, I started asking around. Through word of mouth, I learned about Calgary Immigrant Women's Association and their bridging programs. In 2019, I applied and was accepted as a participant in CIWA's Links to Success program, a bridging program that helped immigrant mothers hone their job searching skills. It came with a guaranteed three-month internship.

I was selected for a position at the University of Calgary's faculty of social work. I worked with Elena Esina, the manager at Shift: The Project to End Domestic Violence. I was excited to be part of a team that did such meaningful work. Regardless of how small my role was, I knew I contributed to the team's achievements, and this was my inspiration to go back to work. If Elena hadn't taken a chance on me, I would have never been on the career path that I am on now.

With my work experience in hand, I was ready to join the workforce. And then came COVID-19. And once again, I was confronted with my old friend: failure. But with some words of encouragement from my mentors, I picked myself back up and applied, applied, applied.

My career counsellor at CIWA, Julia Alexander, told me, "Don't apply for all the postings. Apply only to the organizations you really want to work for."

After eight months and roughly 100 applications, I finally got exciting news. Due to the growing demand for healthcare workers, I got a position in administrative support with Alberta Health Services (AHS).

After 12 incredible months with AHS, I decided it was the right time to look for jobs in the health and safety field again. I had just completed my advanced certificate in occupational health and safety and was itching to learn more on the job. After applying for countless jobs in the field, I received the call I had been waiting for since arriving in Canada.

"When can you start?"

Some people are hired straight away. Some people have the right connections. Many other, like me, must strive to get to where we want to be. We face many trials and tribulations, often with a smile on our faces. Every failure taught me something. My advice to anyone starting out on this journey would be, to own each failure, learn from it, pick yourself back up, and say, "Thank you, next please!"

21

THE POETRY OF THE LIFE OF AN IMMIGRANT WOMAN

KELLY KAUR

My name is Kelly Kaur. I am an immigrant. I am a woman of color. I am a writer. Once, I was afraid to speak up. Here is my journey to my voice.

I was born in Singapore, where the sun sits high in the sky and shines its warm rays on a robust multicultural society. My neighbors were Malays, Chinese, Indians, and others from around the world. We were mostly Asians, our ancestors came from China, India, or were the original Malays of Singapore. We spoke our beautiful languages, all of us connected by Singapore's official languages of Mandarin, Tamil, Malay, and English. We all learnt English in school, this legacy of British colonialism obvious in the fabric of our lives. We had a striking Singaporean accent and spoke Singlish, where we combined our assorted words and accents from our intriguing backgrounds; then we threw in "lah" or "hoh" or "why you so like that one there" in many of our conversations. But it was all ok. It was who we were. We understood each other, got along most of the time and ate the most incredible food from all our miscellaneous backgrounds. We lived in a landlocked island, had the best economy, and lived safe and secure lives, mostly in high-rises dotted all over Singapore.

Then I came to Calgary, Alberta, Canada as an international student. I found out that to be an immigrant is to forever be caught up in an insider-outsider dance. Overnight, I became a visible minority in Calgary. I was, clearly, an outsider, on the periphery of life. I had moved from a comfortable Singapore life to a confusing Canadian one.

As I looked around at my classmates, I felt different. My color was different. My accent was different. My mannerisms were different. My food was different. My expectations were different. Simply, I was different. I didn't understand the basic notions of four seasons for many, many months. And there were all the questions people asked: "Why did you come to Canada? Where are you from? Where is Singapore? Are you Chinese?"

Today, I am a veteran immigrant. But the poem below expresses the original viewpoint of a Singaporean and, perhaps, any new immigrant who feels the disorientation of being a stranger in a new country. Food becomes a metaphorical, symbolic, and literal emblem of loss and reinvention. Some immigrants feel loss through yearning for the familiar food of the country left behind of that exact ingredient, taste, and familiarity absent.

This poem below is going to the moon: It will be included in time capsules in the Nova Collection of the Lunar Codex – Nova-C mission (June 2022) and the Polaris Collection – Griffin mission (Fall 2023). I am grateful to make it to the moon, as a woman of color, as an immigrant, as a writer. It is testimony that all voices are equal and that anyone can find expression. Today, this is my immigrant power that I reclaim and stand by – the power of words, the power of creation, the power of poetry and stories to show the landscape of absence and alienation that immigrants may feel.

A Singaporean's Love Affair

I utter in clandestine code
Nasi lemak, mee rebus, mee siam
Paratha, mee pok, char kway teow,
Biryani, nasi padang, rojak, char siew pao,
Roti john, mee soto, popiah, putu piring
Embedded in my genetic soul
Ravenous for the familiarity of
a satiating sustenance
a childhood defined
a hungry rebellion usurped
a displaced gluttonous immigrant
lost in a gumbo of new worlds
a legacy of bewilderment
longingly relishing fuel
that coursed through my veins
I prattle my mindless mantra
Durian, satay, ice kacang, kaya, teh tarik
Ketupat, laksa, lontong, dosai, agar agar
Putu piring, wonton mee, chili crab
Bak kut teh, chendol, gado gado
A foreigner
Forever famished

I came to Calgary as an international student because of my intense desire to be independent. I wanted to rise above the traditional expectations of a woman whose culture and background dictated and specified traditional roles of women. In Calgary, I was grateful for I found my power through my education and my degrees. Initially, when I arrived in Calgary, I wanted to hide because the path was riddled with challenges. However, I quickly found out that as an immigrant, I must reinvent myself, recreate myself, hold on to what I want from my other life, assimilate, understand, be open, learn, move from invisible to visible, fight for my rights, stand up to racism, sexism, live a dual life of negotiating the best and the worst from one tradition, culture, country and harmonize it with my new country.

I knew that an education would empower me. I am grateful for my degrees. Mind you, it was not free. As an international student, I paid my dues – one and a half times more than what Canadian students paid. My father in Singapore worked tirelessly to support my ventures at the University of Calgary. The price for an education was literally sky high as my father also had to negotiate the exchange fees from Singapore to Canadian dollars. It was a high price for my family. I hold my degrees close to my heart. The rewards are that I have ensured that my Canadian-born son and daughter have university degrees so that they can carve their own paths and independence.

As an immigrant woman of color, I found that my university degrees gave me the voice, power, ability, courage, and opportunities to be successful. The poem below is in a travelling exhibition in North Dakota for the International Human Rights Arts Festival, from January to November 2022. This is my song for all women to be given their freedom and independence to express their true selves. All immigrant women must rise up. All women must rise up.

Women Rising Up

When I was born
my father placed me at the familiar altar of patriarchy
I ranted and raved. Stomped, screamed, and shouted
until reluctantly, my father's infinite love gave me
powerful degrees, one for each hand

When my daughter was born
I breathed intense joy into her lips
carved words of power onto the canvas of her skin
propelled her ahead of lines of dissent
deconstructed dialogues of traditional expectations
celebrated her strength and her passion
whispered in her ear that Barbie was too skinny
and no one needed to wear high heels
unless they wanted to
let her embrace her glorious size, perfect shape, and seamless
color
showed her the map to female autonomy
from lessons learnt in classrooms and on the streets

And she became
sassy, feisty, intelligent, vivacious, beautiful, dynamic,
spirited, confident, audacious, bold, adventurous,
self-sufficient, wise, brave, broadminded, inquisitive,
ambitious, savvy, liberated

We all need just one advocate

Rise up for our mothers, sisters, and daughters

Rise up for the oppressed, muted, and nameless
Rise up for invisible women of the world

until on her own
every single woman in the universe

Rises up for herself

    As immigrants, some of us may face racism in Canada because we are considered visible outsiders because of the color of our skin. We often dance in two worlds – one from our birth land and the other from the country we immigrate to. We often dance to belong to the center. Sometimes, we are pushed to the periphery. As immigrants, we want to simply exist. I don't want to be identified as brown, different, an outsider, from another country. I am proud of being an immigrant. I am proud that Canada is my country. This is part of my poem, published in the International Human Rights Art Festival, New York, January 2022, that speaks of the dreams, visions, hopes and desires of immigrants in Canada.

Still
Still
Still in the silence
We dream of roving ancestors
travelling descendants' dreams accumulated
from all bends of the universe
Of the endless race for unanimity
Of tender words to dress profound wounds
Of the magnificence of diverse shades and vivid

tongues
Of colorful hearts that love indiscriminately
Of discordant minds that connect peaceably
Of anthems of courage and love
Of accents that chant a chorus of harmony

I am honoured to wear my own skin
I am gratified to wear my own skin
I am proud to wear my own skin, eh

It's been a long journey. This is the poetry of my life as an immigrant woman. I think of my country of birth, and I am hungry for food because it defined and shaped who I am. I believe in the power of an education because it recreated and reinvented equal opportunities for me as a woman. I embrace my skin and color because it is my heritage and authenticity. I am a proud, proud, proud immigrant woman. My voice will never be silenced.

22

JOURNEY TO THE WEST

KEWEN WOOD

After all these years of seeking adventures and freedom, I have finally realized that's not what I'm seeking. Instead, it's myself I'm looking for, and how to make peace with myself.

I'm Kewen, made in China. I'm from the golden triangle of communism – my home province Jilin, is next to Russia and North Korea. My reason for being in Canada wasn't always clear to me and has changed over the years. Initially, I would tell people I came to study. But as more people asked, my answer started to shift.

In 2013, I landed in Vancouver with two suitcases – my second trip out of China, and the first step ever in North America. My first trip was as a poor 19-year-old student. Only later I would realize that trip to Europe had been a turning point in my life. I was in Poland for a month, part of a volunteer program doing cultural exchange in elementary and junior high schools. The following month, I traveled through eight European countries by myself. My backpack was jammed with instant noodles and soda crackers. I was a young adventurer! And I wanted to see more of the world.

So, when my application for a scholarship was successful, I headed to Canada to do a master's in geology. I studied uranium mineralization mechanism in Regina – the "centre of the universe." (If you have seen the movie *Deadpool*, you will get this joke.) Regina was also where I met my soulmate (who became my husband). He was another reason I stayed in Canada.

The third reason for staying in Canada, is freedom. I once considered moving back to China, with my husband, after our graduation, but decided not to.

Some people have the misconception that mainland Chinese live under great suppression by a cruel regime. The reality is that for the most part, ordinary people are living ordinary lives, quite happily. But what did bother me about living there, was some of the traditional conventions and societal norms, especially for women. There are expectations for what I can or cannot do, what I should look like, how much I should weigh, who I should marry, and when I need to bear a child. These are my obligations to society and family. Why can't I just be me?

I experienced much greater freedom being a woman in Canada, so I stayed and rebelled against the values and norms I grew up with. I got tattoos, married a Canadian guy, and we became DINKs (dual income, no kids). It would take me a while to discover that being a woman in any country isn't easy. To survive as a minority and a woman in the male-dominated mining industry is difficult. There is a well-established old boys club culture.

Getting a job wasn't easy, especially when competing with local graduates with established networks and intern experiences. At the time, I was hiding behind the resume of *Karen Wood*, to at least get a chance for an interview.

After working for a while as a Superstore cashier and a dishwasher in a nursing home during a mining downturn, I got my first real industry job as an exploration geologist. I was the only immigrant on the team.

I was so anxious during the onboarding process that I could barely speak a full sentence in front of everyone. The other newly hired co-workers seemed so confident. I felt small and weak. *How am I going to fit in? Will they like me? Maybe if I try hard enough, at least they won't hate me,* I thought to myself.

I made a point to follow sports I didn't watch, and I collected slang words and jokes, because I wanted to fit in. It took me a while to catch up with the physical strength required for the job, moving, and lifting heavy boxes. When highly mineralized, a box of uranium drill cores can weigh 80 lbs. For weeks, while the other employees called it a day at dinner time, I worked till midnight. I felt so slow, and I didn't want to fall behind.

Walking alone from the core shack to the camp in the pitch dark, worrying about possible bear encounters, I thought of giving up a million times. But I couldn't face the thought of having people thinking that Chinese are lazy and weak, and that immigrants are not able to work on par with Canadians. So, I stayed. And I succeeded, even being promoted to supervisor later, still the only immigrant woman in the company.

And I did have some fantastic adventures over the years: holding high-grade uranium ore close to my body, hiking in northern Utah looking for copper, trucking around in Montana for sapphires, flying in helicopters over B.C. glaciers, and stumbling through the northern swamps of Saskatchewan.

At one point though, despite the adventures, I felt there was something missing. I was unfulfilled and wanted to have a bigger impact. I realized I didn't know myself. I was lost. A lot of soul searching followed, trying to find my next purpose. So, two years ago, I left the industry in which I'd spent a third of my life.

I have no regrets. Every roadblock has taught me how to get up, dust myself off, and move on. I am tougher and stronger than ever. I know I can work hard and overcome any obstacle. I'm back in school, studying for an MBA. And I am no longer hiding behind the name of *Karen*. I am proudly and confidently *Kewen*.

I never thought I would get married and end up staying in Canada when I started my journey as a student. I explored and made decisions each step along the way, even when things were uncertain.

As first-generation immigrants, we excel at navigating ambiguity, don't we? We learn to adapt to change. We learn a new language, both linguistically and culturally. We try to fit in while not losing our roots. We learn to be okay with straddling two worlds and to be okay with being 'an outsider' in both.

"You are more Canadian than Chinese now," are words that sometimes seem to be a compliment. But sometimes they also hurt. Immigrants are strong, brave, and adventurous. We have all established new lives from scratch in a once strange country that we now call home. We didn't give up when we ran into difficulties. We tried and tried to fit in, wanting to be accepted. Then, we finally realized that we needed to accept ourselves to find peace. Freedom is found inside us.

23

Because my Mom Believed in Me

Larissa Ramazanova

My mom likes to say that it is my husband Vadim to whom I should be forever thankful for bringing me and our eldest daughter to Canada nine years ago. Indeed, my husband's professional experience and hard work in the oil industry allowed us to become welcomed immigrants in this wonderful country.

But what my modest mom never shares, is her own role in this. She has, throughout my life, encouraged me to try new things. She built my self-confidence and encouraged me to venture into the unknown.

As a little girl of five, she let me walk to the bakery to get fresh bread for the family. If I met a friend, it would take me an hour to get home, instead of 10 minutes. No child in our neighborhood could resist the urge to tear into the crusty side of a warm just-baked bread. By the time I got home, only the middle section of the loaf remained. My mom would get a little angry and send me to the bakery again.

At age eight, I started attending music school. Four times a week I traveled across town alone changing buses twice. Squeezed between adults, I had to make sure I reached the doors in time to not to miss my bus stop. While I did love the music, it was the laughter and socializing with girlfriends that were most important during my seven happy years at music school. But I do still love playing the piano, and sometimes I play my mom's favorite piece of music – the sad polonaise by Oginski Michal, "Farewell to the Homeland."

When I turned 21, I graduated from university and was offered a job in the nearby town. What a feeling! I packed a small bag of belongings and 20 packets of instant noodles (my only food for the next two weeks, as my parents did not have much money) and caught a bus. Two hours later I arrived at the tiny town of Aksai. But while I had managed to find a job, I had not arranged a place to stay. With no internet or Airbnb, I walked through the town asking people for help.

"Excuse me, I am looking for a place to stay," I would tell strangers in the street. "Do you have a room to rent?"

Less than two hours later, I was sharing a new apartment with a lovely woman.

That first job lasted for almost seven years, until I met my husband and moved from my country (Kazakhstan) to Azerbaijan, where he lived. My experience of international communication and cooperation at a large oil and gas company was a real eye opener. I longed to live in a country with a fair society and high quality of life.

Many immigrants to Canada face difficulties and feel overwhelmed during the early years. Our family was lucky. My husband was offered a job in the Calgary branch of his Norwegian company. His company paid for our flights and helped us with a hotel and a rental car for the first month after we arrived.

I remember being at Heathrow Airport, waiting for our connecting flight to Canada, and suddenly realizing that our immigration was no longer a dream. It was finally happening! I burst into tears.

My five years in Azerbaijan were stressful: I could not find a good job, I did not speak the language, and the corruption I witnessed was distressing.

As I cried happy tears at Heathrow, our little daughter Liana joined me. There were two elderly ladies sitting in front of us. They turned, smiled, and said to my husband: "It's always hard to deal with women." This made me laugh and lifted my spirits.

We arrived in Calgary, and I do not remember a single day when I felt uncomfortable or unhappy in this wonderful city. Some people call Calgary a village – we live a simple life here. What makes life meaningful and happy for me, are smiling, respectful people, a strong, helpful community, a huge fleet of volunteers, green parks, public libraries, honest police, and a healthy society. Those are the reasons my family came to Canada. We treasure all of it!

Nine years after arriving in Calgary, I still have much to learn, and there are so many goals in my personal development plan. I would like to speak fluent English. Last year I celebrated the fact that I started to enjoy reading in English – my second language. I would love to make friends among Canadians from different ethnic groups – currently most of my friends are Russian. I plan to study and land my dream job – to be an education assistant in special education.

Calgary is our beloved home. Now and forever. Every morning I walk my middle daughter to school under the waking Calgary sky, the most beautiful sky in the world, and I feel blessed. There is so much I love here: long biking trips in Fish Creek park, joyful gatherings with friends in my backyard, shovelling snow on frosty winter days, breathtaking views of the Rocky Mountains from the hiking trails, roaming among the bookcases in Shawnessy library.

I believe I can overcome any challenge and hardship. Because my mom had every confidence in my ability to succeed. My mom has never come to Canada to visit us. Ironically, she is afraid to take such a long trip and to travel by air.

I called her last week. She doesn't hear very well anymore, so I need to speak up.

"Hey, mom," I almost shouted. "It's Larissa. I just wanted to thank you for always believing in me and letting me go. I love you very much, mom."

24

RED BALLOON

Maria Divina Gracia Tanguin-Galura

Baguio City, Philippines

F ilipino Sundays meant early morning mass. But for eight-year-old me, it was the chance to choose a balloon. After the service my father would buy me and my two siblings something from the vendors outside the church. This didn't happen all the time, so it was a big deal the day I got a red balloon. I tucked away those happy memories and told myself that one day I would have a party shop.

My entrepreneurship journey started early. In my second-grade classroom, I sold candies out of my mother's olive-green Tupperware sewing kit, the candy sections lined up so colorfully. The white and brown chocolate pillars went quickly, but the purple ube pillars were the bestseller. I walked to the market on Saturday morning to shop for the week's offering. It was fun and made me so happy. Once, my classmate requested lollipops, so I listened. The day my teacher arrived to find everyone with lollipop sticks in their mouths, my business was shut down: it was apparently a major distraction. *Lesson 1: Product placement and timing is key.*

In high school, I would wake up an hour early to fry beef patties and assemble burgers. I walked to school at 7:15 a.m. carrying a sando bag. At 9:40 a.m. it was recess. I only sold to my classmates until girls from other classrooms lined up in our homeroom. I had many repeat clients. Again, I was told by my teacher to stop. But this time, I was directed to drop the goods at the canteen. They would sell on my behalf, and I'd collect money after school hours. With no commissions. *Lesson 2: When opportunity knocks, open the door and say hello.*

In university, I sold balloons and flowers: single balloons on sticks for student organizations; small daisy bouquets for singing grams and sweet nothings. I launched potted tulips and sold these to my professors and the dean. In the Philippines, tulips were watered by ice cubes and were a cool Valentine's Day gift. I sourced my balloons from Divisoria, Manila, and with them I created huge, bold bouquets. My February was planned around peak sales and my engineering classes. With calculated risk, and to maintain a smooth production schedule, I would skip a few classes. *Lesson 3: Planning, resource alignment and constraint management are key for a high stakes operation.*

Upon graduation, my friends thought I would open a party shop. I didn't. I told myself calculus, operations research and statistical analysis were difficult courses to pass.

"Only for me to sell balloons? I don't think so."

I started as an apprentice for a semiconductor company doing time study. I went on to become the only female warehouse foreman in the raw materials department of a paper mill. I went back to the semiconductor company as part of the startup team for a three-part manufacturing plant. I got my masters. I loved all of it.

In between it all, I got married, and my husband and I applied to become permanent residents of Canada through the Alberta Immigration Nominee Program. My godmother sponsored us. It took three years.

Calgary, Alberta, Canada

The grind of daily life: work-chores-camping-shoveling, repeat. Fortunately, I had a little extra time, so I started a side hustle for fun. After selling leftover party supplies from my daughter's first and second birthdays, I started a party in a bin in 2015.

"This is my childhood dream!" I said to myself. "It's happening!"

I used my morning CTrain commute downtown to email clients, checked in at lunchtime and then again at the end of the day on the CTrain home. After two years of doing this, I was swamped and exhausted. At the same time, I was enrolled in a continuing education course at the University of Calgary twice a week after work. Waiting for the train one night, my eyelashes were heavy with ice in the -30°C on 7th St. and 7th Ave. I asked myself, "Why am I doing this? Does this make sense?" I still had to prepare a party bin for a morning pickup. "Oh yes," I tried convincing myself. "It makes me happy and one day it will make sense."

In downtown Calgary, my exercise after work was walking from 7th St. to 1st St. and then taking the train northbound. I fell in love with Stephen Ave. It is where I saw my first Beakerhead robot in the fall of 2015. So when, in 2017, I saw a call for Beakerhead submissions – a festival mashup of science, art and engineering – I wondered about my crazy dream of balloons spilling out of buildings.

Balloons in tow and 38 weeks pregnant, I presented my proposal during Valentine's week. It was approved! In September my team and I executed "Nucleation, an Ode to Bubbles." The following year, I did "Dreams Never Die" inspired by "UP House" for Beakerhead. I was 12 weeks pregnant.

My daughters are now 10, 5 and 3 years old. On weekends, they help me sort balloon bags. Sometimes they stay up late while I install balloons at malls or they help to pop balloons on the street. Will these be memories they will someday cherish? *Lesson 4: Family first.*

I pay tribute to my Filipino heritage by naming balloon installations based on Tagalog words. I name them based on my journey, and chapters of my life, happy or tragic. Lessons 1, 2 and 3 from my years in commerce have come in handy, but lesson 4 was the most important.

The key to happiness lies in those genuine feelings of bliss we experienced as children. Like my childhood memory of family Sundays, looking forward to a single red balloon. If that worked, then what could a thousand balloons do?

It takes grit, resilience, patience, positivity, and an open mind to chase your dreams. I had to look back to where I came from and go from there. Initiative is key. I had had my dream since age eight, but at age 30 I knew I had to work on it. Confident in my traditional corporate abilities and career, I went on chasing my childhood dream. I am now 40 and very grateful and proud of learning to ask for help. *Lesson 5: Ask for what you want.*

It takes all of oneself to invest in a dream to make it a reality. It is worth every second.

People had told me that immigrants can never be as successful in their new homes as they were in their countries of origin. It is not true. In fact, a new country can make you more confident. The culture, values and outlook of your old country are your roots. Canada adds a layer of bold perspective encouraging you to go for it!

Canadians, lend a hand to newcomers. It gives us a sense of belonging. Friends, support your besties. I still keep in touch with my burger and balloon customers. I am grateful to my university friends who helped me carry bags of balloons on the streets. Partners, say yes. Today, I have thousands of balloons, ready for installation. My husband smiles along. Siblings, be the cheerleaders. My sister helped me to pay for balloon supplies and my brother carried tulips to school for delivery. They made me feel so supported. Parents, let your children choose. Support their happiness and encourage even after failure. My father bought me that first red balloon, and my mother let me walk alone to and from the market. Without them I wouldn't be in this position today.

My father died in a car accident in 2004 but I think he would have loved the thank you postcards I sent my clients: each had a photograph of a giant red helium balloon in the middle of the road along Lake Minnewanka Scenic Drive, embraced by trees and greeted by the Rockies. A full circle offering love and happiness to the world.

25

FOTOGRAFÍAS

MARIELLA VILLALOBOS

M y earliest memories of Santiago de Chile are a series of close-up photographs bursting with color: the pink roses in our neighbor's garden; my grandmother's tiny kitchen leading back to the yard where black grapes hang down ripe from the trellises; the bougainvillea that grows across our roof and spills down to hang over the door in a riot of purple; the cool green shade of the trees we would climb in the plaza and the bamboo growing along the right side of the lawn; the golden-orange of ripe apricots, fallen around my bare feet.

Photos did not figure much in daily life; cameras were rare. They seemed to be reserved for important subjects: weddings, or the portrait of a serious, bespectacled man who wasn't family but given pride of place in my grandparents' house (who I would later learn was the late Democratic Socialist president Salvador Allende). This meant that many images of my early childhood were caught only by the imperfect lens of memory.

I wasn't born in Chile. Being a babe-in-arms when my parents left Calgary mere weeks before the 1988 Winter

Olympics, however, I only knew Canada as the land of my birth. Santiago was home.

Life consisted of whatever was in front of me in the moment: trying to keep up with my brother and his friends, playing outside from morning 'til sunset, school. Rain in the winter, uninterrupted sun haze in the summer. Fireworks in the plaza at Christmas. Adults made decisions and rarely paused to explain what was going on. This resulted in many moments where I had to piece the incomplete picture together and make sense of it as best I could.

I didn't know what was happening the night the midwife arrived at our house to help my mother give birth to my younger sister. My brother and I were merely told to stay in our bedroom, quiet and out of the way.

I also wasn't told what pollution was – why it stained our white stuffed animals grey, or why it kept me home from school on days where the air quality was too poor.

When I expressed a wish to be an artist at the age of three, I wasn't told that my father had his own complicated past with my grandfather's fear of the arts as a path to homosexuality. I wasn't told that he had his own graphic design education derailed by the 1973 military coup. I was only told that "if you're an artist, you'll starve your whole life and you'll only be famous after you're dead."

Strangely, this didn't seem to come from a place of coddling my innocence; if I voiced pickiness over food, I was told that "the Uruguayan rugby team that crashed in the Andes had to eat their own dead teammates, so you'll eat what you're given."

When my parents decided to move our family back to Canada, I didn't know that it was a difficult act for my father, who had returned to Chile from a life in exile following the 1973 military coup, and was now leaving it again so we could grow up in a country where your surname didn't determine your access to education. I also didn't know that while packing up our house my mother had suffered the miscarriage of an unexpected pregnancy and needed to be taken to the hospital by ambulance due to blood loss.

Instead, I struggled to picture a country which I had heard adults talk about, but never seen: a place where we could, apparently, wash our beige Peugeot and not have pigeons poop on the windshield that same day. A place that was called Canada from the outside and Calgary from the inside (no one had explained the geography to me either). When I tried to imagine it, the images were in black and white, with only the familiar people and objects rendered in color.

We arrived in Calgary after extensive delays and a fourteen-hour flight via La Paz, Bolivia, from a warm Chilean spring day to a frigid Canadian night. It was dark, colder than anything I had ever felt. The first image of Canada I now had was my aunt's basement, dimly lit with electric light, and the mattresses on the floor we would be sleeping on for the next two weeks.

Even years later, this image of Calgary as a place leeched of color remained. Houses were invariably dark; many had fake wood paneling inside, or chocolate brown paint. Trees did not invite climbing, and even when you found one that did, your landlord would get angry and try to cut off the lower branches. Bad dreams and night terrors were now a regular occurrence.

I suddenly found myself out of step with other children around me and tried to fit in by dulling down my own colors. I wasn't ashamed of my culture, per se, but I resented when people around me tried to make me "speak

Spanish" on command. My mother chose to go back to full-time work and my father stayed home to take care of us, making us different yet again. I didn't see his unwavering love and reliability in the homemade sandwiches I would take to school every day, just that they didn't look like the processed-food lunches of my classmates. I resented the principles that somehow meant I couldn't have all the things that other kids seemed to get from their own (often distracted) parents: branded clothing, expensive birthdays, sugary cereal.

As the bullying started, I grew less and less confident in my own self, my body and hair that didn't conform to beauty standards; I became almost entirely introverted. I hid behind baggy t-shirts (a defensive rejection of femininity) and my intellect, and while I was fiercely proud whenever my parents would sing onstage at school events, I still hadn't learned how to take that strength for myself.

Over time, however, my father finally began sharing glimpses of his experiences during the dictatorship, and those previously resented principles finally began to take root. The more I learned, the stronger the sense of pride in my identity and intolerance of injustice became. I began to embrace the political education he had always provided, consciously rejecting the pressure to fit in and accepting that who I was couldn't - *shouldn't* - be hidden. I chose to value the friendship of those who got me, and shrug off those who didn't. It would still be years before I learned to own my femininity.

Looking back at the images of my childhood now, their sharpness and detail has dulled, much like the rare photos of that time have become blurrier with age; the drug store-processed color seems to fade with each passing year.

Meanwhile, my life in Calgary (and later, Glasgow) offers flashes of vibrancy I never would have expected from either place during the struggle to adapt.

I find myself caught somewhere in between. Those early snapshots are a part of me: the smell of chirimoya fruit (exotic, perfumed), the damp of winter in Santiago (laying the towels on the gas heater before a shower so they might be somewhat dry when getting out), the taste of my father's sopaipillas on a rainy day (slightly sweet, the fried dough almost scalding). And yet, when I return to Chile as an adult, my father and other family members refer to me as "Canadian." It stings unexpectedly, but I can't really argue. My identity is a type of double-exposure: some parts discernible, never fully resolved. I think of Violeta Parra's poem "La Exiliada Del Sur" and wonder what it must be like to feel so much part of a place that your very body is a part of the soil.

When my father dies, I feel like the photograph has been torn in half, the absence more painful than any remembered bullying. I am not only grieving for who he was (a genius singer and charismatic Renaissance Man: the embodiment of reliability and courage), but also the broken connection to the Chilean me. I find myself repeating his history, moving to a new country - Scotland this time - and becoming a stranger in a grey city once again while I try to tell his story in paper and ink. Here I am, an artist despite his wishes, fulfilling a promise to myself and looking for answers. (Would he still have been proud of me?)

My art school professors are at best polite and at worst completely dismissive of the story of a country thousands of miles away on the coast of South America, and a family on the eastern side of the Canadian Rockies. I complete the work; my earned strength armors me against their indifference. I am searching for my culture, and for the complete picture of myself. No pieces missing, even if the whole is still in development.

Someday, I hope, I may even find it.

26

INTERVIEW WITH MYSELF

MARINA YULPATOVA

A s an immigrant I have often had to answer the same questions again and again. My Canadian friend with a Chinese background was born and grew up in Canada as a third-generation immigrant. Despite her perfect English and radio voice, people often expect her to talk with an Asian accent due to her appearance. For me it is the opposite – I look like a local, but when I start speaking, I usually see a surprised look on people's faces because of my Russian accent.

I have decided to write my story to answer the questions I am often asked, as well as the questions I keep asking myself.

Where are you from?

This is the question I am most often asked.

I was born and raised in USSR – a country that no longer exists. Ironically, the city where I lived also does not exist. I was born in Gorky, named after the famous Russian Soviet writer Maxim Gorky. In 1990 the city was returned its historical name Nizhny Novgorod. It is a beautiful city, located at the junction of the Volga and Oka Rivers, like Calgary, located on the banks of the Bow and Elbow Rivers. Unlike Calgary, Nizhny Novgorod is far from any mountains, but its nature has a modest charm: lakes, rivers, forests, hills, and parks. An ancient fortress Kremlin, the jewel of the city, it stands proudly on the banks of the river Volga.

What brought you to Canada? Was it a difficult decision to leave your home country?

Our decision was easy and spontaneous.

After "perestroika" started in USSR, many scientists went to work abroad. A friend of mine settled in San Diego with her scientist husband. She found a job at the University of San Diego, where her husband was working as a research scientist. In 1998, after 7 years in the USA, my friend sent me an invitation to visit. It seemed a miracle – but my husband and I were granted visitor visas! After 10 days I told my husband, "We have to live here."

When we returned home, everything was dedicated to our new dream. We played a lottery to win a green card. I applied to all possible jobs abroad, even interviewing with Microsoft. Finally, we learned about the professional immigration program to Canada.

What impressed you the most during this life-changing trip to San Diego?

The smiles, politeness, fresh air, wide freeways, and space.

In 1998, California was not as crowded and traffic not too bad. We were so impressed with our friends' big homes, and their life comforts. They made our one-bedroom apartment in Nizhny Novgorod seem so tiny. Our garage in Nizhny Novgorod was not even close to our apartment, so my husband had to take a bus to get our car from the garage, and it was dangerous to leave our car on the street at night – it could be easily stolen. By contrast, the beautiful La Jolla neighbourhood in San Diego felt safe and calm, garages were attached to the houses, the streets were clean streets, and the grass in the front yards was neat and green. It created a sense of peace and tranquility.

"This is how people should live," I said to my husband.

Did Canada disappoint you?

Not at all!

My husband, our nine-year-old son, 10-year-old fox terrier, and I arrived in winter. The chinook welcomed us with +15C weather, but in the second week, Calgary showed us how cold it can be. The kind owners of our bed and breakfast helped us to rent our first duplex.

After living in apartments our entire life, we were so happy to have a backyard where our son could play hockey in winter and basketball in summer. We loved our neighborhood, West Hillhurst in the NW: everyone was kind to us, and our son could walk to school without any fear.

Was it difficult to adapt to a new life? What major challenges did you face at the beginning?

I worried more about my husband and son than about myself.

I spoke fluent English, and I had done a lot of research beforehand. My husband felt pressure to provide for us financially. His English was far from advanced, and his first job in construction involved tile setting. For a civil engineer from Russia, this physical job was not easy, and I worried about his health.

It was hard to see my son standing alone in the school playground during lunch break. Kids did not play with him – he did not speak English. He was not invited to birthday parties. But we still felt optimistic about our future. We were a team – each of us had a role and we focused on supporting each other.

What do you miss the most about Russia?

I miss my friends and Russian culture.

Now I know many people in Calgary and beyond, but my best friends are still those from childhood and high school. I am very happy that my son has found a best friend here in elementary school. I hope their friendship will continue throughout their lives.

I miss Russian theatre, museums, architecture. The city where I lived was 800 years old and it kept its historical beauty. I hope someday to visit Moscow and St. Petersburg as a tourist and go to the theatres, museums, and exhibitions. Due to present political issues, I don't know when I will be able to visit my home country again. I hope it will be possible sooner rather than later.

Besides the accent, what was the hardest thing about learning English?

Using "a" and "the" article.

I still don't understand when to say "a" and when "the" and why we need them. Articles do not exist in the Russian language.

What would you say to someone who is thinking about immigration?

Don't let your fears stop you.

Immigration greatly expands your cultural horizons and gives you an unforgettable life experience. Our immigration gave us the gift of a second life. My life is divided in two: life in Russia and life in Canada.

My Russian life was longer, but today I feel that, finally, I can fully enjoy my Canadian life. We came to Canada when I was 39, and my husband is 9 years older. We had to start over completely. We had to study English and look for entry-level jobs. It was challenging and sometimes frustrating, but it made us feel young and fresh again, and motivated us to move forward. As a result, our life now looks anything but boring. Overcoming obstacles gave us a huge sense of accomplishment.

After 18 years living in Canada, do you consider yourself Canadian or Russian?

I feel confident in the Canadian business environment. I feel respected and accomplished as an IT professional.

In my private life I am still a Russian woman living in Canada. I watch mostly Russian movies, read Russian books, and outside of work I prefer the company of Russian-speaking friends. We share a love of the same foods, we sing the same songs, we read the same books.

At the same time, I feel that Canada is my true home, and I am very grateful to this country for everything that happened to us here.

27

---◇---

MY CANADIAN DREAM BEGAN IN THE WINTER

MARTINA MUKETE

"O Canada! Our home and native land." These words remind me of home – Cameroon, where I was born and raised. Cameroon's anthem begins: "O Cameroon, thou cradle of our fathers." Somehow, this makes me feel connected to both these countries.

As a little girl, growing up in rural Cameroon, in Central Africa, I dreamed of living in a big city someday but never imagined it might be Calgary, Canada. My family moved to Canada in September 2010, and Ottawa became our new home. I came to Canada as a young adult, full of ambition and determination to succeed. Canada was the promised land compared to Cameroon, where there were so many limitations for youth to fulfil their dreams. The possibility of getting a job after graduating for most young people was very slim, whereas in Canada you could work and attend school simultaneously.

I've always loved Lao Tzu's words: "The journey of a thousand miles begins with a single step." When I was accepted at the University of Ottawa in January 2011, it felt like the beginning of my journey.

My parents couldn't afford to pay my tuition fees, so I signed up for a student loan. Besides the financial insecurity, and adapting to a new climate, there were other challenges. I questioned my identity. Who was I? There was the fear of the unknown. I felt lost – that I didn't fit and wasn't accepted.

I'd first questioned my identity in one of my university classes where the teacher asked us to introduce ourselves to our peers in small groups. I found I couldn't think of anything else except being African. This question will intrigue me for years as I find myself in Canada.

Fear of the unknown wasn't a new feeling: I'd experienced it when I moved to China before coming to Canada. But this time the fear was so overwhelming that I couldn't express myself in most of my classes. I felt lost, and scared that if I spoke, no one would understand my accent.

Financial instability was my parents' greatest concern. Without jobs, they feared we might not be able to afford food and shelter. We didn't have a car, so we used public transit, waiting for hours in the cold to catch the bus.

I tried my best to create networks with my peers and professors, as everyone emphasized the importance of networking in Canada. I learned about Canadian culture, history, politics, socioeconomics, and geography. Most of my friends were from immigrant families, from all over the world. We shared our moments of culture shock after arriving in Canada and it was great to connect with people from different backgrounds.

I was on a mission to succeed – in my studies and career. During my first few months in Canada, the public library became my haven. I borrowed books, printed documents, and browsed the Internet. To get Canadian work experience, I volunteered at events such as "WE Day," and with the school board and women's shelter in Ottawa. I made use of every service offered to new immigrants. I registered at World Skills Employment Centre in Ottawa, where I learned to tailor my resume and apply for jobs.

I applied for a position as a student senator in the House of Commons (Parliament) and was turned down because I was a landed immigrant. I was confused that they'd reject me even though I fulfilled the requirements of being bilingual, and a permanent resident. But after weeks of grumbling, and researching the process, I discovered that this was a valid point. In the process, I also learned a lot about Canadian history and government.

After completing my degree, I sent out so many job applications, but was unable to get even a cashier position. Reality began to hit and I was getting desperate and frustrated. My Canadian dream was dying. I panicked, crying about not getting a job.

I reflected on my parents who had been unable to find jobs in their respective fields after coming to Canada, despite both having PhDs. And here I was – with a Canadian degree – facing the same challenges. My parents told me not to give up. We – their children – were their Canadian dream. Our success was their pride.

"Even if we do not succeed," my mom said to me one day, "our hope is for you to succeed."

In 2017, I moved to Calgary, Alberta, with the hope that, if one province (Ontario) didn't open doors for me maybe another one would. And doors did begin to open!

I got a few contracts with the private sector as a records technician and an administrative assistant. I went to school again and took the healthcare aide certificate, hoping for a long-term job with benefits. I got a job right after I graduated from Bow Valley College and was satisfied for a while. I started searching for jobs in my other fields of study while I worked as a healthcare aide to pay my bills and student loan.

It took me years, but I finally got a job with the federal government. This was a big relief for me and my family. It was my parents' dream to see me achieve this milestone: a single step in the journey of a thousand miles. Sometimes the steps are haphazard but that doesn't matter. My Canadian dream is gradually beginning to make sense and I am so grateful to be living it here.

28

My Journey

Melike Tasdelen

Everyone knows that it's not easy to leave your country and start a new life somewhere far away. I have gone through so many difficult situations in Canada. There were many hardships, from not finding work to the language barrier. But I want to share my happy experiences, not the sad ones. My journey has been amazing, despite the difficulties. I consider myself fortunate to be surrounded by so many great people and friends.

I was born and raised in Turkey. Growing up, I fantasized about having my own house. I love my parents and siblings so much, but the movies I watched probably influenced me. I believed that real independence meant living far away from your family. It develops your confidence.

In the community that I am from, it is unheard of for a woman to leave her family and move to another country on her own. We tend to value women by the family they create and the kids they birth. We judge them by their husbands' jobs. Those were some of the cultural norms I grew up with. So, for me to move to Canada by myself was considered extreme. My friends and family were extremely critical of my journey.

My family is not very traditional, yet they believed that women could not live alone. My mom always said she would not be happy until I got married. So, part of my reason for moving to Canada from Turkey was to prove that I could live independently.

I was very young when I arrived in Calgary, and filled with excitement, wonder, hope, and positivity. However, it was not long before the excitement was replaced by financial worries. I was not from a wealthy family, and I needed to cover my own expenses. I needed work, but I was a student with a tourist visa. I did not have a work permit. After a couple of months, with only a couple hundred dollars left, reality hit. I was desperate. Through the help of a friend, I found a job in a restaurant, working "under the table." I believe many immigrants go through this. It supposedly makes us resilient.

There were so many obstacles. I struggled to get my degree because I had to work at so many odd jobs to pay my tuition. With no family around, I was homesick and lonely. The long, frigid Calgary winters did not help. I was vulnerable and found myself in toxic relationships. I wanted to feel safe and not alone. This feeling of being alone was the most challenging part of my journey.

Along my journey, though, I met some amazing people. I made great friends and always found people willing to help me. I got permission to pay my tuition fees in installments, which was not customary for the school. That allowed me to finish my studies. I made a beautiful friend who opened her home to me when I needed it.

To get by, I took on an array of different jobs. One of these was working in a Calgary motel as a receptionist. I worked there for almost four years, and during that time I met so many people I would probably never have met if I had not left Turkey. I witnessed a drug overdose. I had to hound my employer after my paycheque bounced. There was a police incident with arrests and guns drawn. I felt as though I was in a Hollywood movie.

I also worked at a banquet hall for a while. When the bartender quit, my employer asked me to bartend for a while. I did not even know the names of the drinks. My friends and family in Turkey did not drink, so I didn't even know the different types of alcoholic beverages that existed. When people asked me for a scotch, I had no clue what to give them. It was so embarrassing. But eventually, I learned.

I consider everything that happened to me a blessing. From those early days crying, to the days filled with happiness, this has been an incredible journey.

Today when I look at my life, I see only beautiful memories. I see the progress, know the commitment, and appreciate the people around me. I am grateful. Being an immigrant is not easy. I feel as though I belong to two cultures and two countries. Canada has welcomed me and provided me with equality and opportunity. Turkey is my origin. Canada is my home.

29

YOUR NAME WAS JANEZ AND YOUR NAME WAS JOHN

MIRIAM FABIJAN

I called you Ata, and I called you Dad. I remember sitting on your lap when I was four or five years old, listening to your many stories, ones you never tired of telling. There was no other place I would rather be than happily nestled in your arms.

You spoke in stories; most of all you liked to reminisce about your life in Slovenia. I loved that you wanted to share your memories, your journey with me, but I sensed that you buried yourself too much in the past. Rarely did I hear you speak of what today meant to you, except for family. Family was everything to you – especially when we all sat around the kitchen table telling stories, joking, and laughing. You loved it when we were all together.

For hours I would sit with you and listen to how your life had unfolded. When I was older, I would get frustrated when you would constantly repeat those stories. When I was older still, I started to realize that by repeating them you were trying to heal yourself from the many traumas in your life, and to make sense of your life and the decisions you had made. If I let you go deeper, I would always be rewarded by learning something new about you, something you had never talked about before. I sat close and listened.

Your early childhood in Slovenia seemed wonderful, magical, even though you had to work hard and had many chores. Your family farmed and you lived off the land. Though you were not very well off, you seemed happy. The small village of Zgorna Besnica was your home, high in the foothills, surrounded by fertile farmland, rain forests, tall mountains, a rich history, and many generations of your family. You lived a stone's throw from the church whose bells you learned to ring, calling to the people who lived there.

I was just six years old when you first took me to Slovenia, the birthplace of your stories. This trip gave your stories life, made them more vivid, gave them colour, sounds, tastes, smells, and, most importantly, faces. You brought me back to the family that had been lost to us by distance and time. The hours of playtime with my cousins and the warm hugs from my grandmother filled my heart. (I have since visited Slovenia six more times, on my own and with my husband and daughters, and always made to feel at home.)

You were very young when you were sent away to live with your uncle, a priest who lived in Ljubljana. He was called Janez, and you were named for him. There, you continued your studies, excelling in drafting and engineering. You were the second oldest of nine, and you always knew that you were expected to leave someday to make your own way. You were just so young when you did. I don't know if I would have been that brave.

As you finished your studies, World War II broke out and tiny Slovenia (then part of Yugoslavia) was invaded by the Germans, Italians, and Hungarians. These occupying forces set out to erase your people, their identity, their politics, and their culture. Young men were randomly selected for destinations unknown. You told me you did something silly, not taking the situation seriously enough, and you were sent to a concentration camp. It almost killed you. (I think it did kill you in the end. Those five months of sleeping on a cold floor allowed rheumatism to take hold of your muscles. Even after all the hours you spent sunning in our backyard, you could not rid yourself of this affliction. Eventually it crippled and weakened you, and it was in part responsible for your passing. You held off the consequences of this physical trauma for as long as you could. You were ninety-three.) You never told me what happened in that camp. It scares me to think of what they might have done to you.

Somehow your uncle found out where you were and got you out, but then you faced the most difficult decision of our life – return home or leave. Your mom told you to leave. She wanted you to live; she loved you so much. But this meant that you had to leave without saying goodbye.

I think you always questioned that decision. Had you stayed, they would have made you fight like they did your brothers, to kill perhaps – something you could never have done – or be killed. You relived this time of your life by telling your stories to whoever would listen. I don't think you ever fully moved past it, your childhood home, leaving; you clung to those memories.

You told me that when you got on the transport truck to leave Slovenia, the one meant to take you and others to safety, you sat at the very back of the tarped cargo bed. You were watching the road to see if the driver made the right turns. You knew these roads, and you were ready to jump if you were being lied to. Luckily, they took you to a DP camp in Italy, and you officially became a "displaced person." You stayed in several of these camps for four years, working, living, surviving, hoping, and dreaming of being able to make a home somewhere.

Eventually, Canada let you in. This meant more transport trucks, trains, a long boat ride across the Atlantic, arriving on the east coast of Canada in Halifax. When the immigration officials asked you your name, you told them it was John. Not Janez. You believed it would help you fit in better in your new country, so you anglicized your name.

You made your journey with very little: a wooden suitcase and a trunk. (I have these now; they are my greatest treasures filled with memories and mementos of you.) Another long train ride followed, taking you as far away as possible from where you started. This would be the best way you could imagine making a fresh start. You got off at the last stop possible, Lethbridge. There you met mom, another Slovenian so far from home. (She made a similar journey, but her story is even harder to tell.) You shared with each other a common language, culture, dreams, and traumas. You gave each other love and made a new life together. You were married for 63 years.

I was the last of your four children. I completed the family you had always wanted, and I would not be here if you had not risked so much. You named me Miriam, meaning beloved, waited for child.

The two of you built our home in Calgary, never tiring from hard work, always keeping busy, motivated to make a wonderful life in your new country. You both learned a new language, your first one slowly slipping away. I always found it curious that as the years progressed, I rarely heard you speak Slovene with each other.

I was told you had a thick accent and that you were difficult to understand, but I couldn't hear it. You tried teaching me your language, but I was not a good student. I had always struggled in school, and I brought those struggles to our lessons. I was easily frustrated, and sadly our lessons ended.

Ata, when I was little, I did not fully grasp what you were teaching me through your stories. They were just adventures. Only when I was older, did I understand the many adversities you faced. I may not have learned how to speak Slovene, but I did learn resilience, faith, kindness, a love for family near and far, a respect for the past, the desire to honor where we came from and the strength to move forward no matter how difficult. I will always be thankful that you made sure our family here in Canada stayed connected to our family in Slovenia. I call both Canada and Slovenia home. For that, I thank you Dad!

My name is Miriam, and my name is Mirijam.

30

_____ ◆ _____

LIFE AS IT HAPPENS

SAAWAN LOGAN

I am the youngest of three girls and was born and raised in Fiji, a small island nation, where asking for help was okay and helping someone was never an imposition. My parents raised us to believe that girls could do anything in life and we were responsible for own achievements. With that, we were given a voice and the tools to survive whatever life brought.

Life in Fiji was very simple and, in our family, quite difficult. We did not grow up with much and some days it felt like we were barely scraping by. At 15, I took over our family business so we would have a roof over our heads and food on the table. I later immigrated to Australia and in my twenties, love brought me to Canada.

As a child, leaving Fiji for "greener pastures" was not unusual. What was unusual was the thought of what life would really be like once you started unpacking in your new home.

New beginnings are always exciting but never easy. It is such an optimistic feeling, and it makes challenges look like tiny stars in a faraway galaxy. But holding on to that optimism is one of the hardest things I ever did.

Moving far from family, friends and loved ones, and starting over again from ground zero, is like being born again. You get to relearn about yourself – the hardships you can and cannot endure, the strengths you have. Oh, did I mention a new language? I was fortunate to be fluent in English when I moved to Canada, but I did not understand slang. As a nonnative English speaker, I only knew "proper" English – what I had been taught in school and read in books. I still remember the roar of laughter when I said I had great eyesight and did not need spectacles.

"Spectacles! Who uses that term?" said my friend. "It's glasses."

I had a lot to learn.

My confidence took a huge blow when I learned that I could not work in Canada. It created the same insecurity I faced as a 15-year-old, who did not have the financial means to meet her family's needs. Coming from a family where financial challenges were a daily reminder, I had always envisioned that having an undergraduate degree in accounting was my golden ticket to evergreen employment. But I was told that without Canadian work experience or education, my chances were slim.

I had left Australia filled with such confidence. But it was being replaced by deep insecurity, and the feeling of not being good enough. The only way to overcome this was to constantly remind myself of all that I was fortunate to have.

I was confident in my language skills even if I had to learn to speak "Canadian." I knew I was resilient and still had the fire of a 15-year-old who was going to do whatever it took to build a new life in Canada. I spent my time volunteering with charities that I was passionate about and that became the start of an amazing life in Canada for me.

I became part of the corporate world, passionate about our industries, our politics, and our social issues. I found myself cheering for the Canadians in the Olympics and proudly sang "Oh Canada" in my Fijian accent. I wanted to showcase my love for my new home to the world and kept thinking of ways to bring Canada to the rest of the world. Canada became home. I became Canadian.

In 2020, I left the corporate world that I loved so dearly to start my own business. I co-founded North Water, a company with a goal of putting pristine Canadian spring water on the map. North Water was my way of eliminating plastic pollution while introducing the world to our great Canadian water. With North Water, I found my passion and an avenue to tell my story. This was my way of giving back to the country I was so proud of.

There is so much to be proud of as an immigrant. It is not just our courage to pack up and move to a new country, but the spirit and hope we bring for a better tomorrow. And then there is our ability to reach the heights of the corporate world and perhaps even create our own corporate world. One with the ability to change our lives and perhaps even the lives of others.

All of this came from knowing that it is okay to be vulnerable and to ask for help. And some day, we might be able to help someone else. Life is a struggle but focusing on the wins and being okay with all that does not go our way is what makes us who we are.

When we are lonely and have no friends, when the winter jacket isn't warm enough, when we are lost on the cold streets running late for a job interview and cannot find the way, when nothing seems to make sense, we need to look for the same optimism that helped us pack up and leave all the familiar comforts. What seems like a hardship is just the beginning of a new chapter that exposes our strength and character. Before we know it, we are the ones providing directions to those who are lost.

31

LANTERNS ILLUMINATING MY FUTURE

SHINOBU APPLE

Ten years ago, one early August evening, I stopped by the Olympic Plaza in downtown Calgary, to check out the Floating Lantern Peace Ceremony. I sat on a bench in the centre of the park, watching children and their parents having fun in the large pool, pouring water over themselves.

Reflecting sunlight and splashes of water glittered in the air and children squealed with laughter.

It was a beautiful summer moment.

I had come to honor my great aunt who was killed on August 6, 1945, in downtown Hiroshima by the atomic bomb.

A woman I'd met previously at a church event approached me.

"Hi there! Nice to see you again! You know how to make paper cranes, don't you?" Karen was the program director of the Ploughshares Calgary, the organizers of the event. She had remembered me from the event the previous year.

"Yes," I replied. "I know how to make paper cranes."

"Great! We need someone to teach attendees how to make them." She pointed out the table under the tree at the west side of the park. And that's how I got involved with the peace group and the Floating Lantern Peace Ceremony in Calgary. Ten years later, I am now co-chair of the committee.

June 2021 found me at Olympic Plaza again, to look at the condition of the park. After the prolonged pandemic shutdown, parts of the park looked deserted. I sat on the same bench I'd sat on 10 years earlier and reminisced about the past.

In the early '90s, I left to study in the U.S. I was 30, and my age was one of the reasons I left Japan. Even though it was nearly the twenty-first century, people in Japan believed that women only had commercial value until 24 or 25 years of age. Like a Christmas cake that goes stale, a woman over 26 had no value in marriage marketing platforms. My parents, hard-working business owners, believed this too. They wanted their daughters married before their 26th birthday.

I respected my parents deeply, but watching their own rocky relationship, I did not believe that marriage would bring me happiness. If I married, it would be purely because of social pressure. After two of my younger sisters got married, my parents labeled me with 'lack of filial piety.' Because of this social pressure, I felt choked by my lack of freedom to decide my own future including whether to marry or not.

I also remembered an old photo of my great aunt which was enshrined inside a Buddhist altar in my grandparents' house. The altar was situated in a special room, in the darkest part of the large old house. My grandma kept candles and incense continually lit on the altar. This created a mystical atmosphere.

One summer, when I was in elementary school, I snuck into the room and found an old white and black photo of a beautiful young woman. She was smiling. I asked my grandma who she was.

After a moment's silence, Grandma told me it was her younger sister. She had married an engineer and they had relocated to Hiroshima for his job during WWII. Both died during the atomic bombing in 1945.

"Shinobu," she said solemnly, "Promise not to share this story with anyone else."

I promised. I have never forgotten the serious look on my grandma's face that day. Only in adulthood did I understand why I had to keep it a secret: death by atomic bomb carried a huge stigma for the families involved, so they never wanted it to be known publicly. Radiation was believed to be contagious, causing birth deformities. It would have been fatal blow to any prospective marriage if people in the community knew the great aunt's death was due to the atomic bomb. So, both households told people that my great aunt and her husband had passed away in Tokyo during the great Tokyo air raids. In this way my great aunt died twice: first by atomic bomb and second by hiding the true cause of her death.

Marriage should be a personal decision, not decided by social pressure. I was lucky to be able to relocate to a country where there was no pressure on me to marry. For almost 10 years, here in Calgary, I have volunteered for the disarmament of nuclear weapons. I am passionate and tireless in this. Why? Probably because I want to challenge something that people think unchangeable: the unchangeable adherence to "the nuclear deterrent" and to "the social pressure on women." I remember the beautiful smiling face of my great aunt in the old photo. I can honor her and carry on her legacy by unwaveringly walking this path for peace.

As the summer afternoon became evening, the sky in Olympic Park turned a beautiful rose-pink color. A familiar voice called, "Shinobu! Have you finished here?"

"Yes, Jim. I have," I replied, standing. "Thank you for coming to pick me up."

As the breeze touched my cheeks, I turned and walked towards my husband.

32

WHEN I FOUND MYSELF, I FOUND CANADA

SHIVI AGARWAL

B orn and raised in India, I was the first one in my family to migrate overseas with no friends or relatives. Struggling to find a thriving environment in India, I dreamt about carving a genuinely happy life on the other side of the world. My dream of migrating to Canada finally became reality in 2019.

It all started when I was working in Chandigarh, India. I had an opportunity to interact with the community of AIESEC students and started dreaming of exploring the globe and building a more meaningful life abroad. AIESEC is an international student organization that helps students worldwide live and work in different nations and gain experience. During my three-year tenure, I lived with people of 26 different nationalities. The experience was unparalleled. I felt a sense of belonging and alignment between our thought processes which helped me to see beyond the barriers of my society.

My family, however, was unwilling to uproot for this journey, and I was emotional about leaving them behind. I tried to enroll in higher studies, but financial barriers stopped me from pursuing international education in

Canada. Residency was also not an option at that time. So, I made peace with life in India. I experienced love and heartbreak. When I separated after a long-term relationship ended, I hit rock bottom, suffering from depression and anxiety. My mother, father and brother encouraged me to take a solo trip, to get me out of my depression.

I sometimes think about how we are often so close to the solution we are looking for, but because the solution scares us, we avoid it and look elsewhere. For years I avoided my truth and was consumed with mistrust and lack of self-confidence. The loss I experienced shattered me until I got the courage to dream about what I wanted, my life in Canada. I used to talk about this broken link that left a dark space in me filled with answerless questions. I am proud to have a family that gave me the confidence to fill this space with words of empathy.

This part of my story is called realization. I gathered the courage to overcome the psychological barriers that stemmed from my past toxic environmental conditioning. I changed jobs and cities and started fresh with the confidence that my parents gave me.

I was doing well in my career and headed the academic training department of an MNC (TATA Group) and was happy to perform at par with my standards. Still, I did not feel I belonged, and my calling for Canada surfaced again. My only chance now was to immigrate. It was 2017, so a lot had changed over the years, and this time my parents supported me.

I registered myself for anything remotely related to Canada – like business chambers and corporate meetups in Delhi. It was time to act and make my dream a reality. I kept a map of Canada in my bedroom to manifest my way there. I talked to people and organizations who could either give me employment support letters or guide me with the settlement process. I filed for my immigration, but my age was a hindrance. I applied through PNP (Provincial Nominee Program). Unfortunately, my job was not in demand. Despite the obstacles, I did not lose hope.

In 2017, while working with TATA Group, I received an email stating that the Canadian Prime Minister, Justin Trudeau, would be visiting India with his delegation, and my company was the platinum sponsor for the event. At the same time, a business chamber I belonged to, ICBC (Indo-Canadian Business Chamber), invited me to participate.

I was thrilled. With my glass in hand and business cards in my pocket, I attended those events with one thing on my mind: network! I talked to as many people as I could about establishing business relations between India and Canada. I exchanged contact information and afterwards sent emails, festive wishes, and LinkedIn messages. Getting tired was not an option.

After clearing the French language assessment, I gained some more points, and by mid-2018, my immigration scores had fallen below the cut-off, and my file was picked up. Sheer happiness! Wasting no time, I contacted the connections I had made two years earlier. Someone from the delegation party responded, offering me a job in Calgary.

I landed in Calgary in April 2019. My employer greeted me at the airport with flowers and helped me with accommodation at SAIT, which allowed me to familiarize myself with the city. I arrived on Sunday and started work on Monday. I know I was fortunate to have employment before landing in Canada. This is quite rare for newcomers.

My first job in Calgary was with a start-up, and I was their first international hire. The experience was unparalleled. During my transition from a newcomer to a known face in Calgary's marketplace, I got the opportunity to help hundreds of job aspirants build capabilities and connections to achieving their career goals. Driven by passion for engaging in community development programs and the desire to form meaningful social connections, I developed invaluable relationships with professionals and organizations committed to building an economically rich and inclusive society. I have now transitioned from my career as a customer success manager in the tech industry and am working with a tech start-up in Calgary.

Gandhi once said, "The best way to find yourself is to lose yourself in the service of others." I feel a responsibility to give back to the community and explore ways to serve outside my home and the workplace. I am glad to have invested a significant amount of energy in understanding Calgary's socioeconomic trends, cultural viewpoints, and the start-up ecosystem. My love for the city and its people inspired me to get involved with The Startup Impact Project. This is a dream project inspired by fostering entrepreneurial culture and igniting a growth mindset through transformative stories. My talk show brings conversations with some of the most innovative and insightful entrepreneurs, investors, business leaders, educators, and industry veterans to viewers worldwide.

Journaling and literature are powerful tools to express and inspire others. It is a way to reflect and become conscious of the inner strength that helped us through the dark times, understand ourselves better and shape us to become the person we are today for a brighter tomorrow. Fear of regret, the desire to succeed, self-belief and a crazy amount of hard work helped me defy the odds, persevere, and achieve some wonderful milestones. I am imperfect and have fear and self-doubt like the rest of us. But I am determined to bring out the best in myself, keep evolving, have fun and live a purposeful, expressive, and fulfilling life. To close, I would like to share a powerful quote by Charles Bukowski, "Can you remember who you were before the world told you who you should be?"

33

A "Better" Version

Swati Dhingra

At the airport, although my excitement helped calm the storm of emotions and nostalgia, leaving my parents was not as easy as I anticipated. I was ready for the next chapter of my life: moving from the place where I was born and raised to a new place I imagined exploring, while evolving, un-learning and re-learning almost all aspects of my life, but this time all alone.

My journey from a self-sufficient girl from India to an independent self-reliant woman in Canada has been incredible in so many ways. Coming to a brand-new country with no contacts was challenging, but my desire to advance my professional career and my parents' unbound faith in my abilities were enough to get me here.

Being recognized as a skilled professional worker, I was so happy to arrive in Canada as a permanent resident. I remember telling my mom: "It's okay, I can come back anytime. I am just going to explore things. I don't have to stay there forever." Little did I know at the time that this blaze of exploring a new country would transform into a fire within me to re-invent the person I was, to take a spin on my understanding of life, of struggles, of challenges and finally knowing that I was capable of so much more than I imagined.

I relied on Google maps to learn the transit routes. I had never taken transit back home, and of course the snow made it worse. The first challenge was finding a place to stay. One week's prebooked hotel stay was just enough to introduce me to some of the neighborhoods. Walking for miles, missing buses and getting tired of looking for rentals, I realized that my introverted, distrustful approach was not helping me.

Taking the first step out of my comfort cocoon, I started talking to people – strangers! This was never easy for me, but it was the only option when all the people around me were strangers. My first connection in the city was an elderly lady in transit. This led to me finding a place to stay. What a feeling! By simply talking to someone, I found a place to stay and was then introduced to other Indian families who helped me understand Canadian life from an Indian immigrant perspective. I was so happy about breaking the ice and having the courage to talk to strangers. But this was just the beginning.

I had found a place to live, had a few people to talk to, and just enough to live on. But now I had to find a job! Life revolved around visits to the community library, getting resources from immigrant agencies, and working on my resume to make it fit for the Canadian job market.

I went for a number of interviews, with a variety of experiences and encounters. But each time I was told either that I needed Canadian experience, or that I was overqualified for the job, or that my educational credentials were not recognized here. I remember leaving interviews with this screaming question: "How do you expect me to have Canadian experience when I am looking for my first job in this country? How does a new immigrant ever get Canadian experience?"

After a month in the city, I still had no job. I had to turn down some offers that weren't suitable, to wait for the right fit. It was very frustrating, but I was learning to be persistent and tenacious, to rise above dissatisfaction and self-doubt. I tried hard to not let others' opinions influence me or allow me to question my abilities.

Finally, a new chapter began with my first Canadian job! But everything was so different – the office, my colleagues from all over the world, and a work culture I had never experienced. I was a racial minority and establishing myself while showcasing my talents was not straightforward. I needed to prove myself and make the people around me believe in my skills, but I was struggling to understand their expectations in the first place.

After six months of overworking, people pleasing, and saying "yes" to everything, even volunteering, I was feeling constantly stressed. That's when I realized that I needed to be more assertive and not let the people around me make me feel vulnerable. Yes, I was new, and I needed to establish myself, but I also needed to learn to say "no." I re-learnt being patient and that it's okay to take time and allow things to fall in place. Everyone starts somewhere, and this was my beginning.

Encountering the cultural, social, environmental, and emotional challenges of being in a new space was not easy. I had come from a well-supported family where the only decisions I had ever made were about my studies and the subjects I wanted to pursue. From the moment I had landed at the airport in Canada, with no one to meet me, my story as an immigrant woman was all about exploring my inner self with every single experience revealing some untold confessions, some meaningful realizations and showcasing the untapped potential I had within myself. Making so many decisions on my own in a new country (choosing a place to live, rejecting or accepting jobs, making or breaking friendships, and trusting or doubting people who were complete strangers) was transformational.

My immigration journey has been life-changing and has made me stronger, better, tougher, and more confident. Besides the bitter experiences of some important life lessons, I also got a chance to meet some wonderful people who have made this journey more gratifying. With each passing day, I revisit my decision to take on this immigrant journey and feel content: I am enough, I am competent, and all my dreams are valid. Yes, it is challenging, but it is doable!

34

DANCING MY LIFE

TATIANA OSHCHEPKOVA

I will never forget how I loved to dance with my mama when I was little.

My mom and I would dance together to cheerful songs on the radio. My grouchy teenage sister would join us, and soon we would all be giggling as we twirled around our cozy little apartment in Ekaterinburg, a large industrial city in Russia. Mom truly enjoyed dancing, but sadly could never dance with my father, as one of his legs was much shorter than the other. I believe it was because of a disease he'd had as a baby, but I'm not sure.

My father was born right before WWII as the youngest of six children. (By the end of the war two of his siblings had died.) He loved sports. He kayaked and cycled with friends, but he never danced with my mama. He also loved photography and took tons of pictures of me and my sister. I still have those black and white photos capturing some of my happiest childhood moments, including our dance shenanigans. Thirty years later, these photographs are with me in Canada – my new beloved home.

When I was six or seven, my mom took me to the local Ballet and Opera Theatre to watch the Nutcracker for the first time. Everything was so magical, so mesmerizing – Tchaikovsky's music, dancers, costumes, decorations. It was a dream! I think I took in a deep breath when I walked into the theatre and did not breathe out till the end of the show. For weeks after the performance, I talked only about ballet. I asked my mom a million questions about ballerinas: "How do they manage to dance on their toes? What are their tutus made of? How could they turn so many times and not get dizzy?" Day after day, I heard Tchaikovsky in my head and fell asleep picturing myself on that stage in a tutu and pointe shoes. I even tried to copy the ballerinas' moves! I dreamed that one day I would dance like that.

Reality, however, did not cooperate. The closest ballet school was a seven-hour train ride from my hometown. There were some local studios where girls could learn ballet basics and folk dances, but my parents were working full time, and nobody could get me there. Like most people in the USSR, we didn't own a car – in the 1970s this was a luxury. Public transit in our newly built neighborhood was also not great. The biggest obstacle though, was the physical criteria for ballet students: girls had to be a specific height, very petite and slim as a straw.

I was skinny, but I was also very tall and ungainly. With very little adult supervision, we played outside all day in summer while our parents worked, often in construction sites or dumps. I would come home covered in dust, knees and elbows bruised and scabbed from climbing trees and fences. As much as I wanted to be a delicate flower twirling to Tchaikovsky, it was not going to happen.

At school I got selected to play basketball because of my height and athletic abilities. I was not sure if I wanted to play basketball, and be a part of a school team, but the coach was persuasive, so I joined. I did not understand the game, I got yelled at, and my teammates often laughed at me for my daydreaming. They nicknamed me *ballerina* because I used to tiptoe across the field. My coach called it flitting like a butterfly and tried to make me change it to heel-to-toe running, but I never succeeded. Even though I did not enjoy it, I did not like to give up, so I stayed on the team for two years.

My mom and I continued attending ballet performances, and while I still dreamed of dancing, I put that desire on hold – for almost 30 years.

After school, I attended university, got married and had two children. Shortly before emigrating from Russia in 2006, I started dancing with my husband. When we arrived in Calgary, we were both very anxious: we had limited English, limited savings, no income, and limited resources for starting over professionally. We also knew very few people. We wanted to make new connections, find new friends, and enjoy our new life as much as possible. We signed up for dance classes, to meet locals and have a break from the struggles of adjusting to our new life. It was one of the best decisions we made.

My husband and I learned salsa, bachata, and tango. We practiced social dancing, performed with two amateur groups at local festivals, and loved all of it. Even though I was busy raising our children, pursuing new degrees, and building my professional career, I always found time to dance. Dance gives me joy, boosts my energy, and helps me to unwind after a hard day. It is my meditation, my self-care, sport, and social life.

Today I am 51, and I have two grown-up sons and an amazing grandson who recently turned one. For the past 15 years, I have lived far from the country of my birth. Both my parents passed away several years ago. However, every time I step into the dance studio, I feel like that excited little girl at the Nutcracker. I am currently taking ballet, modern, tango, and samba dance classes. It is my gift to my inner child – the one who dreamed of dancing on a big stage. And when I dance, I am back in that cozy little apartment, dancing with my mama.

35

GREEN ONIONS AND GINKGOES

VITA LEUNG

I'm slicing green onions, trying once again to make perfect steamed fish, hoping to hear the satisfying sizzle of ginger-soy-infused oil poured over fish skin, a technique I can't seem to master. It never sizzles.

It's Lunar New Year's Eve. My husband has brought home a three-pound tilapia. A whole fish is required to ring in the new year. Hong Kongers believe that eating a whole fish – head and tail – will bring prosperity at both ends. My husband tells me he fought all the old ladies at T&T, the Asian grocery chain owned by Loblaws, to get us the best one. One of the ladies taught him how to pick the liveliest fish, and how to get the butcher's attention on the busiest day of the year. As always, a story. But apparently, it worked.

I'm on the phone with my mother when he gets home.

"Three pounds is enormous!" she says. "The fish will never cook properly. It will probably be overcooked. You'll have to steam it for 30 minutes, maybe longer, and it's already so late. What time do you plan to eat dinner?"

Anxiety sets in. I want this dinner to be flawless. I have swept and scrubbed away the mold to start the new year with a clean house and a clear mind. I want it to be perfect, so that we can focus fully on the celebration. But I am running out of time. Cooking a complex feast is extremely challenging in our tiny kitchen. I love doing it, but it's not easy. Besides, in Hong Kong this would be considered a luxury kitchen.

I am preparing three traditional dishes, mostly because the names of the ingredients in Cantonese have similar intonations to auspicious words. Ho see fat choy (dried oyster braised with Gobi Desert seaweed), sounds like "good things and prosperity." I am also preparing bau yu and wild bamboo mushroom on siu choy (Napa cabbage). Bau yu is abalone. At $80 a package (eight sounds like good fortune) it's sure to bring good luck. Siu choy sounds like "smiling vegetables." And the steamed fish, yu, sounds like "abundance" – from the beginning to the end of the year.

This year, we're prepared. Instead of drying our own oysters at the last minute like we did last year (what tenacity my husband showed!) we took the advice of a Hong Konger we met at T&T.

"You could just buy ho see at the medicine shop in Chinatown," she said. "It's right under HSBC."

I also stashed away some rare fat choy (Gobi Desert seaweed) from last year, so I didn't have to pressure my mother to mail us more.

Often, when I slice green onions, I think of Popo, my maternal grandmother. The expert way her fingers guided the knife as it made long ribbons, the layers of green onions amassing to the right. Fine ribbons, almost like threads. Something I aspire to. Something attained only after decades of practice.

Decades.

Not just practice but wisdom. Popo had knowledge that had been passed down from her elders, that she'd absorbed from her siblings and cousins, not read from a book, or been taught through a privileged education. School for girls was unheard of when Popo was growing up. A little pile of green begins to form as I wonder: *What's been passed on to me?*

Popo escaped foot binding and was the last generation in our family during which ear piercing for girls was mandatory. My ears aren't pierced because my mother is proud that she was able to choose. But I didn't get to choose. So, when I turned 18, and my mother had said that my body was mine to do whatever I wanted with, I went to Morningside Mall to get my ears pierced. But the sound of the piercing gun scared me so much, I decided not to go ahead.

From my first visit as an infant, I spent holidays in Hong Kong quietly watching, making, and eating food with my grandparents. One summer, I cracked open fresh ginkgo nuts to make ginkgo congee. (The fruit of ginkgo trees is great for the respiratory system and brain health and believed to be an aphrodisiac.) I thought it tasted gross, like dust and dirt, but I would never have said that out loud.

Years later, when I was 18, Popo took me to the street market. I watched in horror as the butcher defeathered the chicken we'd selected for dinner and cut off its head. That's also where I saw frog legs that continued to twitch after they were skinned and detached from the bodies. I decided to go meatless. My iron levels plummeted within a few short months and so my mom put me back on a balanced diet. By the time I saw Popo again, I was back to eating meat.

Popo passed away a few years ago. She spoke Fujianese and broken Cantonese, and I speak broken Cantonese and English. The bits of language we had in common were enough to share simple instructions, but not enough for stories. Not enough for me to truly know who she was. I inherited her beautiful cheongsams, the form-fitting dresses that originated in 1920s Shanghai; old Hong Kong films help me imagine how she might have lived. Perhaps she, like Maggie Cheung, also stepped out in a cheongsam to pick up noodles. Noodles garnished with green onions. Such glamour. Such poise.

As I continue slicing the green onions, I'm angry with myself for not trying harder when I was in Chinese school. Maybe Popo and I could have written to each other. But I was teased for having slitty eyes, for having a name that was unusual, for being a typical piano-playing straight-A Chinese kid, gifted even. It made me hate my heritage – hate myself. In high school, I could have joined the Chinese club, sung Canto songs at a karaoke bar, and learned about Chinese history, but I didn't. I read *Sweet Valley High* and wished I was one of the twins from California. I wasted my parents' hard-earned money during university, doing exactly the opposite of what a serious student would do: clubbing and partying. Maybe if I hadn't been singled out or tried so hard to fit in with the white kids, I would have made different decisions. But then I wouldn't be where I am today.

Today, I'm not ashamed. I respect my heritage. I stood joyfully this year as my husband hung red banners in front of our house to welcome in the new year. I am trying to rip down the invisible walls I have put up and to learn about the past, shout out to the future, absorb western *and* eastern ideas, make all kinds of food, especially Chinese cuisine, learn about Chinese art, language, philosophy.

I smell burning!

Oh no! How did I burn the bau yu? What a waste!

Plumes of smoke fill the room. Crap! The special fish pot has run out of water. Panicked, I lift the fish. I choke from the smoke, scream at my husband. He helps me slide the fish onto the plate. It's ruined. It's going to taste burnt. My mom says burnt stuff gives you cancer. I hate this small kitchen. The whole year is ruined now. It's all my fault.

I throw the burned pot out into the snow. My husband turns on the fan.

"It's fine," he says. "It's still good."

"It's ugly," I retort. "I hate it."

But I must finish what I started. So, I heat the pot and pour in the oil. Ginger next. Ugh, it doesn't sizzle. The green onions go in next. They sizzle just a bit, infusing the oil with their freshness. Hm. Pretty. Beautiful green ribbons. Like my grandmother's.

Maybe dinner will be okay. The smoke has even started to clear.

"Looks good," says my husband.

He's right.

I forget to wear my cheongsam, but it doesn't matter. Dinner is on the table, decorations are up, the house is clean, the red envelopes are ready to give out to the neighborhood kids and tomorrow we'll Zoom with my parents and siblings.

This is going to be a year full of good things.

36

———— ✦ ————

MIGRAINE AND IMMIGRATION: SUFFERING IS OPTIONAL

YELENA SEDOVA

I t would be such a shame to die next to a trash can on Christmas Eve. It was freezing. Trembling, with chattering teeth, I reached into the pocket of my bathrobe and searched for my phone. But I must have left it at home. The neighbors were all gathered in their cozy homes, enjoying the smell of turkey. And I was dying.

But let me start at the beginning.

December 24, 2018, like every other day of the year, started with a headache. I made a note of every migraine in my calendar. By December, only 28 days of that year were migraine-free. Only 28 days when I was able to really laugh and not hide my tears.

I had tried almost everything: medicine, blood tests, so many doctors.

I had tortured every doctor available with the same question: "What is wrong with me and how can I get better?"

"Migraines cannot be cured," they said. "Try these pills."

Nothing helped. My head hurt more and more. I was a fighter by nature, but years of migraines, and immigration, had exhausted me. I had lost this fight. At one point, I became so desperate, I started researching euthanasia. Life was so difficult.

You might wonder what immigration has to do with any of this. Well, I had had migraines before, in Kazakhstan. They would send me to bed for a day, then disappear and only return in a couple of months. But in 2010, after moving to Canada, the migraines increased. At first, I wrote it off to acclimatization, then to the stress of moving, then the constant changes in the weather. The first time I ended up in emergency, the doctor told me that Calgary is sometimes called "the headache capital." Due to the frequent changes in atmospheric pressure levels, temperature and wind, a lot of people suffer from headaches.

Let's go back to 2018, and what happened on Christmas Eve, that beautiful and long-awaited holiday. My husband had taken our son skating. I planned to take a headache tablet and lie down for a while, hopeful that the pain would subside by the time my family returned. As I threw away the package, I noticed that the trash can was full. I decided to take it out. It was -25 C. I rushed through the glistening snow to get to the bin.

Suddenly, my right temple exploded with pain. I grabbed the trash can lid, slipped, and fell heavily on my back. And then there was silence. And darkness. When I came to, I tried getting up, but I couldn't. Only my right arm was able to move. I moved it slowly, millimeter by millimeter, trying to reach the phone in my pocket. It wasn't there. I panicked.

The frost was making its way through my clothes, consuming the heat in my body. The neighbors would be no help: no one would be outside, and I wouldn't be seen from the road. By the time my husband returned, I would have frozen to death.

Suddenly, I was calm. Death in a bathrobe, next to a garbage bin is not how you want your children to remember you. With one functioning arm, I crawled towards the house. It was at that moment that I realized that my pain and my health were my responsibility. I would do everything in my power to ensure this never happened again. I would dig through all the available information on the treatment of migraines. I would try everything and anything to get rid of this pain. And I would never again take the trash out at night.

That day provided a Christmas miracle. On his way to the skating rink, my husband realized he had left his wallet at home. He arrived back to find me – a caterpillar on the ice. At the hospital, they filled me with medicine, felt my head, and sent us home. Thankfully, I had regained all movement.

At home, with tea and Christmas cake, my new life began. It led to years of study, research, trial, error, and discovery. And victory over my migraines.

The most interesting thing was the role stress plays. Immigration is extremely stressful. It changes your life completely. And this discovery turned out to be one of the most critical aspects of recovery.

When you immigrate, there is the stress of losing your social circle. It takes time to meet people and make friends in a new place. There is the additional stress of having to process huge amounts of new information. And to learn new ways of doing things (like sorting garbage). When children get sick, it is hard to know where to go and what to do. Communicating in a foreign language, means listening closely to every word. And then wondering whether people understand you.

And then there is the stress brought on by an identity crisis. Back home, you were perhaps a boss, but here you can't even get a job as a sales associate at a store. There, you belonged to your nation. Here you belong only to your family. There, you were surrounded by familiar culture and values. Here you must adapt to the environment and learn new values.

As an immigrant, you need time to adjust. The stress of it all can result in anxiety, stress, even depression and migraines, as in my case.

It has been three years since that life-changing Christmas Eve. I have been living, not just surviving. I almost never get migraines anymore. I have also been helping others do the same. You can choose whether to lie in black ice hell or move towards warmth and health. I believe that long-term remission is possible. One step at a time.

37

── ◆ ──

MERCI MONSIEUR

ZOONG NGUYỄN

Calgary, Alberta has been our home for 17 years. During this time, I have watched the city grow, with newcomers from all over the globe settling here, just like my family.

From our first home in Montréal, Québec, to today, I have shoveled more than 40 seasons of snow. I don't get excited when snow falls. Nor do I do any winter sports, but I can live with winter as long as I have my family.

With time, the early hardships of trying to integrate into Canadian life, have faded. I'd rather let them go anyway. I prefer to keep only the sweet, tender memories.

I do remember though, how tired and dirty my father was when he came home from work every day. My parents managed a gas station with a garage attached, back when full service was popular and credit card payment was a novelty. My dad's face and hands were always stained with motor oil and his uniform always smelled of gasoline and tobacco.

I have no photos of those times. The only time we took photos was when we were dressed up for Sunday temple. My dad spoke French fluently and he chatted with everyone who came to the gas station. People sometimes stopped by just for a short visit, a cigarette, and a Coca Cola. Today we have self-serve gas stations and mobile devices to keep us entertained in our own homes.

Like me, my younger brother and sisters helped at the gas station after school. In rain, wind, snow, and cold we pumped gas. I was good at mental math and handled the cash. We were often tipped a dime – sometimes a big quarter. A pack of chewing gum cost a quarter then.

In those days, every teenager's dream summer job was to be in the sun, chatting to customers at the gas station, hanging out with other neighborhood kids, buying gum balloons, chips, candies, and slush. We lived the dream. But winter was not as idyllic.

When the car tires rolled over a rubber tube, the air in the tube activated a metal piece that then hit a bell like a bicycle bell. When we heard that sound, no matter how cold it was, we had to go out to pump gas.

"Your turn, Zoong!" my brother shouted.

Sometimes it was "un dollar du régulier, s'il vous plait" – just a dollar's worth. At times it was so windy that the change would be blown from our frozen hands. There were even a few times when customers drove away before paying and we would lose a day of pay.

When my dad heard of a gas station with better traffic and more sales volume, he applied to get transferred there. We moved to a different apartment to be close to his work, and my siblings and I changed schools taking two or three buses to get to class.

Growing up there weren't any Asian groceries. We craved Vietnamese food, but we had to be creative with ingredients that were available in the store.

My parents worked at the gas station for five years and saved enough money for a down payment for our first house, close to another gas station, of course. Two years later my dad was diagnosed with lung cancer and passed away six months after that. My mom was a widow for 40 years until she passed away in 2018, after raising five teenagers in a new country by herself. I never saw her cry or heard her complain, but I know she missed my dad's support.

My mom spoke only a little French, and even less English. She expressed herself more with gestures than words. When self-serve gas stations started to emerge, lots of customers did not know how to pump their own gas. Mom would show them how to extend the hose when the car was too far, and how to hold and squeeze the nozzle to avoid splashing. She used her hands to communicate with gestures, her body tilting toward the car, her mouth speaking multiple languages all at once: "Monsieur, vous uh bóp uh comme ça good."

Everyone understood her.

My mom loved the color purple and had a collection of blouses in various shades of mauve that she wore to the Buddhist temple on Sundays. That was her simple joy: to pray for the family and socialize with the ladies. I wish I could still drive her to the temple and listen to the ladies matchmaking. Such tender teenage memories!

We learned resilience from my mom's hard work and sacrifices. Today all her children and grandchildren are professionals. My daughters did not experience the hardships I did but they understand the struggles. I ensured they spoke Vietnamese, as well as French and English. My parents' legacy is a love of life, and support for one another.

They taught us to work hard and seize any opportunities that came along.

My only regret is that my dad did not live long enough to witness how multicultural Canada has become. The authentic Vietnamese food he used to crave is now served in restaurants in Calgary and across North America. Bánh mì and Pho have become the McDonald's of this city.

We've come a long way, embracing our journey to get here. The humility of serving gas and waiting for little tips was the defining factor for us to get better jobs than laboring and braving the elements. We wanted to *be* the ones giving tips, then hearing "Merci."

My birth country, Việt Nam, is still my motherland but my home is where I hang my hat. My family is all here with me, and my heart belongs to Canada. As long as there are gas stations, I feel good: filling up my car, smelling the gasoline, remembering my whole family hanging out at the 7/11 gas station, and a big 25 cents tip.

"Merci monsieur."

AFTERWORD

ELENA ESINA

Immigration is a life-changing journey of moving from one country to another for permanent residency. It is not easy and one wonders why people do it. This book answers this question and many others in 37 different ways through the voices of women who landed in Calgary from nearly 30 countries worldwide. Our immigration pathways included settlement as part of the economic class (such as skilled workers), refugees, family sponsorships, temporary foreign workers, and international students. In addition, some of us were born in Canada to immigrant parents or moved when we were very young.

As a project manager and co-author, it is difficult to sum up how much this experience has meant to me. First and foremost, I am deeply grateful to Gayathri for inspiring us all through such a collaborative process of developing our stories. I was captivated not only by the diversity of our cohort but also by how transformative the self-discovery process was in reflecting on the stepping stones of the immigration journey. When I read my story aloud for the first time to other participants at Gayathri's workshop, a wave of tears rolled down my cheeks: a mixture of gratitude,

189

joy, relief and an overwhelming aha moment: "I made it! I belong!" I truly felt immersed – as one of our participants, Karishma, says – "in a crockpot of emotions, cooked meticulously and slow."

I am not the first (and won't be the last) to admit that immigration is a challenging journey that requires sacrifice and perseverance. No short story can fully capture this multifaceted experience, but a compilation of stories, such as the ones in this anthology, gives us insights into a bigger picture. Only after savoring every story can we begin to grasp the complexity of this journey and truly appreciate these women for the courage, strength, and value they bring to Canadian society. Many participants described the common hardships of starting from scratch to build a new life. But what struck me most was that almost every story included the word *dream*. These testimonies represent both a love letter to the places we've left behind and a heartfelt aspiration to embrace our home, Canada.

I have attempted to list a few transformative themes that unify our voices, but I know it will take many more conversations to unpack our shared knowledge.

- from leaving everything behind to committing to lifelong learning and growth
- from riding the emotional rollercoaster to adopting healthy coping strategies
- from wrestling with constant change and stress to cherishing the present moment
- from struggling as an immigrant child to appreciating parents' sacrifices and hard work
- from navigating culture shock and expectations to healing self and recognizing intergenerational trauma

- from grappling with loneliness to trusting kind strangers
- from searching for identity and authenticity to rediscovering family and human connections
- from living in two worlds to honoring values and traditions
- from experiencing racism and sexism to advocating for change and building a welcoming society
- from facing inequality and discrimination to helping to dismantle systemic oppression
- from trying to fit in and assimilate to finding belonging and acceptance
- from fumbling to find purpose to giving back and making a difference
- from striving for freedom and security to becoming a proud Canadian
- from surviving to thriving

So what do I hope you will take from these themes? I have two concluding thoughts.

First, for those who just landed in Canada, you're in for a treasure chest of empowering wisdom. I wish I had a book like this when I embarked on my journey! You will face many challenges and injustices along the way that may cause you to feel lost, overwhelmed, or fearful. But remember, you can always come back to this book, read a story or two or the poem, "Where I Belong," and remind yourself, "if she can do it, so can I!" It is an ongoing journey; you may never feel like you've "arrived," but it helps to know you're not alone. Like a caterpillar transforming into a butterfly, you will emerge from the cocoon, use obstacles as opportunities for growth, and unapologetically fly towards your dreams. So, open your heart to let those "kind strangers" help you on your journey, as many participants referenced in their stories. When nothing seems to make sense, think back to the reasons for your immigration. Celebrate your accomplishments – small or big. Hold on to your optimism. Share your experiences and culture with your children because they want to know. They are searching for identity in a new country, and in due course, they will come to appreciate you for connecting them to their roots. Your stories and support will help them make sense of their experiences, just like the stories in this book did for us.

For those of you who have established roots in Canada and proudly call Canada home, I hope this book will help you better relate to the experiences of colleagues, friends, and relatives who immigrated from other parts of the world. Perhaps, you will flip through these pages, and the next time you encounter someone with a different background, you will feel drawn to go deeper than the surface. Because stories have a way of doing that. They fill us with empathy, lessen our fear of the 'other,' and gently challenge stereotypes. They help us find meaning and connection in the uniqueness and the universality of our human experiences. If the stories you read in this book inspire you, leave a note on Instagram @campfire_kinship. Tell your friends about it, and add it to your book club. Better yet, invite us to your organization to host a book reading event and further unpack the transformative themes listed above. Finally, if you wish to create an even bigger impact, contact info@campfirekinship.com to organize a storytelling workshop for your team, highlight diverse voices, or assess where you want to be on your equity, diversity, and inclusion journey. Whether you are a professional who serves immigrant families, an organizational leader, a policymaker committed to change, or even a kind stranger, we all play essential roles in building a more inclusive community for future generations. And if there is one thing I know for sure from the privilege of co-authoring this book, this is the highest aim of storytelling, and I wish for everyone to experience it.

Sincerely yours,
Elena

WHERE I BELONG

HUMIRAH SULTANI

For this poem, each participant was asked to capture the essence of their story in a single line. All responses were woven together to celebrate the transformative moments that have shaped the individual and collective journeys.

I close my eyes
and open my heart
as I remember where I am from.

a familiar land-

where the golden prairies kiss the sun and sky
as the majestic mountains reign the horizon
cloaked in freshly falling snow

where ocean tides hum an eternal cadence
as each wave reaches out further to embrace the shore
always under a sweltering sun or a frigid full moon

where endless forests and a thousand lakes
contrast the vibrant tropics where jasmine blooms

195

while sweet mulberries shrivel under the very same sun.

yet, an unacquainted land-

where communist shoulders crowd my home province
and oppressive hands treat our sisters like Christmas cake,
yet, the deeds of others cannot compromise my love of
big cities

where our people guard the truest definition of freedom
from within our city like the Oxford of the East
to the country described as letters from two alphabets.

I do not dare to look back
like a sunflower of her own volition

for in this new silence, I am finding my voice
guided by the songs and stories of my people
of inspiration and love and a better life

I am tenderly rooted-
by the gentle hands of my mother
and the warmest affections of my father,
showered by the sacrifices of ancestors,
the richest souls in the poorest families-
in that space, between my past and future,
where my struggles have carved a place for me

Triumphantly, I dance and dream of beginning anew
planting my failures into strange soil like discarded seeds
to cultivate my inner turmoil into hopeful opportunities

in this land where I find myself,
I have also found myself.
like petals,
I have been plucked away from my home
thirsting for memories during a never-ending draught

once again, I have planted my roots
but now with a mighty fortitude that pierces stone
as I transform myself
and this place
into where we belong.

ACKNOWLEDGEMENTS

We express our sincere appreciation to Calgary Arts Development for believing in our mission to celebrate diverse voices. This project would not have been possible without your generous support.

To each of our writers - words cannot express our gratitude for placing your faith in us to lead you through this journey. The invasion of Ukraine occurred just as we submitted our first drafts. For some of us, it's a grave reminder of the trauma of war and violence that displaced us from our homelands. Yet, time and again, you reached for the courage to tell your tales. You transcended borders and stood in solidarity with each other. You stuck with the writing and editing process despite varying degrees of comfort. And you did it! You captured a heartfelt snapshot of your immigration experience – just a *glimpse,* if you will (though admittedly, many of us could have written sagas)!

It is no small feat to bring together such a rich and diverse collection of stories, and we could not have done it without the patience and encouragement of our families, alongside the meticulous guidance of our editor, Lindy Pfeil. We are also grateful to Cynthia Cabrera for designing our beautiful cover art, Humirah Sultani for curating our collective poem, "Where I Belong," and Mounira Chehade for her dedicated editing support.

Lastly, thank *you*, our readers, for opening your hearts and minds to learn our stories. If you're inspired by the power of storytelling in action as we are, we invite you to visit www.campfirekinship.com, where a guide to telling your first life story awaits, as our gift to you.

Gayathri Shukla and Elena Esina

ABOUT THE AUTHORS

GAYATHRI SHUKLA (she/her) is the founder of Campfire Kinship (www.campfirekinship.com). She holds an electrical engineering degree from the University of Calgary, and an Executive MBA from Queen's University. A practitioner of human-centered design and guided autobiography, Gayathri helps individuals and teams discover their unique strengths while building empathy. This is her first book, and it introduces you to immigrant women from across the world who have made Calgary, Canada home. Their stories draw on your emotions, making you laugh and cry. And they make you reflect on what it means to find belonging.

• • • ● • ● • • •

ELENA ESINA is an adjunct professor in the faculty of social work at the University of Calgary where she currently manages a large-scale initiative called Shift: The Project to End Domestic Violence. Elena holds a master's in social work from the University of Calgary and a bachelor's in financial management from the Petrozavodsk State University in Russia. As part of her desire to give back, she provides mentorship to immigrant women and has, as of early 2022, hosted work experience placements in Calgary for more than 40 women from all over the world. This is her first book, and she hopes it will inspire, bring awareness, and spread kindness. www.preventdomesticviolence.ca

• • • ● • ● • • •

ADO NKEMKA (she/her) is a musician and journalist based in Calgary, Alberta with a bachelor's in sociology. Her bylines include CBC, *Afros in Tha City*, *Toast* and *Avenue Magazine*. Her work centers arts and culture, identity development, neurodivergence, as well as the subversion of cultural expectations and social norms. She loves interviewing brilliant minds – profiling people, businesses and organizations that value community care.

• • • ● • ● • • •

ADRIANA SARTORI is known for her compassion. Working full time as a business owner and Pilates instructor, her passion is to help others feel better physically and emotionally. As an Italian Brazilian she makes them laugh during exercise so that they forget how hard it was. With her bachelor's in physical therapy, she helps her clients achieve their goals and prevent injuries. She's a loving wife who loves to mountain bike, rock-climb, and paddle board with her husband. www.adirection.ca

• • • ● • ● • • •

AMEN KAUR has a BA in psychology and is a certified mindfulness facilitator, born and raised in Calgary, Canada. She practices mindfulness in her daily life through meditation and creative outlets. Amen is the author of the best-selling children's book *Dealing with My Feelings*, about how to work through difficult emotions mindfully, and *Raise Me with Empathy*, a book on the powerful impact of self-love from a child's perspective. She is passionate about mindful parenting. www.amenkaurbooks.com

• • • ● •• ● • • • •

ANAM KAZIM holds a master's in biochemical and environmental engineering, and a bachelor's in chemical engineering. She has also authored publications in various fields. Kazim was elected in 2015 as the Member of the Legislative Assembly for Calgary-Glenmore. Prior to politics, she spent two years as an applications engineer in the manufacturing industry. After politics, she ran her own honey business as an entrepreneur, and co-founded HoneyVista Inc. Her most recent venture is the creation of her personalized perfume called INTRIGUE. For Anam, integrity is a person's ornament and diversity is the world's jewel. https://www.linkedin.com/in/anamkazim/

• • • ● •• ● • • • •

ANNA ZAKHAROVA is an internally displaced person (IDP) from Crimea, Ukraine who fled from Russia's military invasion in 2014. Anna is a Fulbright alumna with a master's in international studies from Old Dominion University and a master's in community social work, from the University of Calgary. Anna has worked as an administrative assistant with the United Nations Development Program in Ukraine, faculty of social work at the University of Calgary, at a homeless shelter and is presently family school liaison coordinator - Ukrainian. She is an active member of the Ukrainian Youth Association Canada and "Vatra" Ukrainian Dance Ensemble.

· · · ● ·● · ● · · ·

ANUSHA KASSAN was born in Montréal, to a South Asian father and French-Canadian mother. She grew up close to her two younger sisters. She pursued graduate studies in psychology. Anusha is currently an associate professor with a high impact position in child and youth mental health in the School and Applied Child Psychology program at the University of British Columbia. Her scholarly interests are informed by her own bi-cultural identities, and an overarching social justice lens. Anusha's program of research presently includes two major foci: immigration experiences across different groups (newcomer youth, women, 2SLGBTQIA+ peoples), and cultural and social justice responsiveness in professional psychology. This scholarship has important implications for psychology training, practice, and research as well as policies related to equity, diversity, and inclusion.

· · · ● · ● · · ·

BENAZIR RAHMAN, born and raised in Bangladesh, moved to Canada with her husband and toddler in 2020. By profession she is a researcher. Her research interests include international trade, social work, and post-secondary education. She loves to connect with new people and motivate others. She believes in making a difference by giving back to the community. Currently, she is helping Afghan refugees to find meaningful employment.

• • • ● • ● • • • •

DR. CHARLOTTE ANYANGO ONG'ANG'A is a linguist, career development specialist and storyteller. She holds a PhD in linguistics, a master's in Teaching English to Speakers of Other Languages (TESOL) and a bachelor's in English language and literature. Her expert linguistic knowledge is applied in the areas of resume, CV and cover letter writing, networking, interview preparation, job search strategies, and workplace communication. Charlotte has taught linguistics, communication skills and provided career guidance at higher education institutions for over 12 years in different countries. As a hobby, Charlotte enjoys reading and writing memoirs. www.charlotteonganga.com

• • • ● • ● • • • •

CHELSEA YANG-SMITH (she/they) is a visual artist, photographer, and emerging writer living and creating work in Mohkinstsis, Calgary, Alberta. Her current art practice has been thematically exploring their Burmese Canadian heritage and family history through photography, printmaking, and book arts. www.chelseayangsmith.com

• • • ● • ● • • • •

CYNTHIA CABRERA is a contemporary realist painter and designer born in Guadalajara, Jalisco, Mexico. She earned a bachelor's in interior design and later a diploma in graphic design. Currently residing in Calgary, Alberta with her husband and two kids, she has regained full focus on her fine art. Her work infuses traditional realism with a surreal dreamlike quality and could be best described as conceptual realism or narrative symbolism. To get in touch with her, or see her latest work, visit www.cynthiacabreraart.com.

• • • ● • ● ● • • •

EMILY YU (she/her) is a second-generation Chinese Canadian born to Hong Kong immigrants. She writes and dreams on Moh'kinsstis Treaty 7 territory, also known as Calgary, Alberta. She has been published in *Ricepaper* magazine, and her short story, "The In-Between," was selected for the Humainologie Short Story Festival in 2021. Follow her on Twitter @emilyyu_writes.

• • ● ● ● • ● ● • •

GERI LIVELL has always been fascinated with storytelling. Besides fruit and dark chocolate, she loves writing, reading, watching movies, and dancing. Her love for storytelling started with writing in her secret journal, writing letters to pen pals and friends, and writing short stories for fun. Whether with words or body movements, Geri uses storytelling to express emotions and reach people's hearts. Her hope is to inspire others to follow their dreams and find fulfillment in life.

· · · ● · ● · · · ·

HUMIRAH SULTANI is a self-taught multimedia creative based out of Calgary, Alberta. Her canvas includes traditional illustration, digital painting, photography, and creative writing with a special focus on storytelling and reconciling cultural identity. Recognizing the importance of education as a catalyst for freedom, independence, and autonomy, she has cherished every opportunity to learn and perfect her craft. She blends her family's experiences as Hazara Afghan refugees in Canada with her professional work as a pharmacist in pediatric oncology to tell the complex, uplifting, and often heartbreaking stories of her generation.

· · · ● · ● · · · ·

INEZ ASHWORTH, founder of Inclusive Concepts, is a cultural innovator and a trusted advocate with her own unique style. In school she was the one standing up to bullies, making friends with the new kid, and boasting crazy hairs colors. Her life and career have been dedicated to working for equality and justice, bringing people together and creating inclusive environments where everyone can be their authentic self. Much of Inez's energy and inspiration comes from community work, volunteering, and mentoring minority students. She counts herself lucky to be one of the people following their dreams.

· · · ● · ● · · · ·

JESIEBELLE SALCEDO is a Filipina Canadian teacher, reader, and writer based in Calgary, Alberta. She holds bachelor's degrees in Canadian studies and elementary English as an additional language from the University of Calgary. To date, she has worked with many first-generation and immigrant youth in local non-profit settings and within the school system, fueling her passion for anti-racism education. In her spare time, Jesiebelle enjoys baking up a storm, exploring new foods, creating pottery pieces, and spending time with her friends and family.

· · · ● · ● · · ·

KAREN DURHAM is of Anglo-Indian origin. She immigrated to Canada from Dubai, U.A.E. in 1997. She has lived and studied (secondary and post-secondary) in Calgary ever since. She is a registered yoga instructor, writer, and artist. She loves to learn about her family roots (stories and traditions) and about other cultures through travel. Her newest role is wife, and she looks forward to creating stories with her darling husband.

· · · ● · ● · · ·

KARISHMA SUTAR is a budding poet who loves to express herself through writing poems. Writing for her serves as healing and an opportunity for reflection. She has written extensively about her family members and friends, expressing her admiration and gratitude. Her loved ones receive poems as birthday gifts, which she personalizes by adding details about their strengths, achievements, and journeys. She often adds humor and has a knack for beautifully expressing her emotions and feelings in words. She hopes to continue this passion for writing and to create blogs in the future.

●●●●●●●●●●●

KAZLINDA KHALID was born in Kuala Lumpur, Malaysia, and is a first-generation immigrant. She spent eight years in Glasgow, Scotland, before moving back to Malaysia to attend high school. She studied law at the MARA Institute of Technology and became a qualified lawyer in Malaysia. Currently, Kazlinda is an occupational health and safety specialist with an international logistics company and is excited to see where her path takes her. Pre-COVID, she enjoyed travelling the world with her family, and during the lockdown, she learned to play guitar badly. Kazlinda lives with her husband and three children and is proud to call Calgary home. www.linkedin.com/in/kazlinda-khalid/

●●●●●●●●●●

KELLY KAUR grew up in Singapore and lives in Calgary. Kelly teaches at Mount Royal University and Athabasca University. She has been published in Qatar, Italy, Malaysia, Zimbabwe, the United Kingdom, Singapore, Canada, Berlin, Prague, Australia, India, and the United States. Some works have appeared in *New Asian Short Stories 2015*, *The Best Asian Stories 2020*, and *The Best Asian Poetry 2021*. Her poems have been published in the International Human Rights Art Festival in New York. She has been published on UNESCO's Cities of Literature website. Her novel, *Letters to Singapore*, was released on May 1, 2022, by Stonehouse Publishing.

· · • ●· ● • • ·

KEWEN WOOD is a strategic sourcing specialist for ETCH Sourcing Ltd. based in Calgary, Alberta. Born and raised in China, she immigrated to Canada in 2013. Kewen is a lifelong learner. She holds a master's in geology and is an MBA candidate. She actively advocates for equity, inclusion, and social responsibility at workplaces. She aspires to help newcomer women to liberate, feel belonging and find inner peace. www.linkedin.com/in/kewenwood/

· · • ●· ● • • ·

LARISSA RAMAZANOVA is happily married with three daughters. She landed in Calgary as a new immigrant in November 2012. In 2021, after being a stay-at-home mother for a decade, she started an educator career with the Calgary Board of Education. Though her job as a lunch supervisor gives her much joy and satisfaction, she plans to become an education assistant in special education. She loves working with children and believes that all kids deserve happiness and a quality education.

· · • ●· ● • • ·

MARIA DIVINA GRACIA TANGUIN-GALURA migrated to Canada with her husband Terry in 2011. They are raising three daughters in Calgary and enjoy weekend trips to Banff for fun. Maria's bright smile is reflected in her numerous delightful creations for the community. In September 2022, it will be five years since her first balloon art installation. She is thrilled to do more across Canada. www.calgaryparty50.ca

· · · ● · ● · ● · · ·

MARIELLA VILLALOBOS is an award-winning illustrator, graphic designer, and lecturer still straddling two worlds – currently Calgary, Canada and Glasgow, UK. She graduated from the Alberta University of the Arts' visual communication design program in 2010 and completed her master's in illustration at the Glasgow School of Art in 2019. She can be found in cinemas, right up front at concerts (due to her height), playing piano and bass guitar, bingeing historical and cultural documentaries with her partner and their cats, and trying to visit every country she possibly can – often specifically to try their food. Find her at www.townofwolves.com.

· · · ● · ● · ● · · ·

MARINA YULPATOVA was born and raised in Russia. She graduated from Gorky State University with a bachelor's in applied math and started her career as a computer programmer. After working for 17 years in the Institute of Applied Physics of the Russian Academy of Science in Nizhny Novgorod, she moved to Canada with her family in 2004. She received a business analysis certificate from Mount Royal University and continued her IT career as a business and systems analyst in higher education institutions. Marina likes to travel, read books, and write short stories. Her hobbies include watercolor painting, ikebana, yoga, and Pilates.

•••••••••••

MARTINA MUKETE holds a bachelor's from the University of Ottawa with a major in public administration, an Algonquin College diploma in journalism, and a health care aide certificate from Bow Valley College, Calgary. Martina works as a program assistant with NSERC. Prior to joining NSERC, she worked as a health care aide at St. Teresa's place (Covenant Care) and at Agecare Glenmore. Martina loves art (painting) and is also the author of *Beautiful Scars*, a poetry collection on Amazon.ca. Art is therapy and medicine to her soul.

•••••••••••

MELIKE TASDELEN moved from Turkey to Canada by herself after graduating from accounting in 2013. She also has a degree from the Southern Alberta Institute of Technology and works as an accountant. She recently married and enjoys singing and hiking.

•••••••••••

MIRIAM FABIJAN is a Calgary-based artist. Her artwork is autoethnographic. Her focused research and creative explorations are founded in her cultural heritage, personal narratives, self-reflection, and social insights. Her search for a sense of place, lineage, voice, language, and identity are central to her work. Fabijan has exhibited her artwork extensively across Canada and in Europe, including in Ljubljana, Slovenia in 1992, a year after Slovenia became an independent country. Instagram: @MiriamFabijan

• • • ● • ● • • • •

SAAWAN LOGAN is the founder and CEO of North Water. She has worked across Asia Pacific, Australia and more recently, Canada. She spent most of her career in oil and gas and has always had a keen eye for a business opportunity. Saawan started North Water as a pledge to end plastic pollution while bringing to the world pristine, Canadian spring water. She enjoys spending time in nature, travelling and cooking. Saawan is involved in the community and volunteers with initiatives where she can make a difference. She believes in hearing everyone out and providing meaningful opportunities for everyone.

• • • ● • ● • • • •

SHINOBU APPLE, PhD, is an author, independent researcher, and translator. Her research interests are Buddhist meditative practices, Buddhism and women, engaging Buddhism for social change and peace building. She volunteers as co-chair for the Floating Lantern Peace Ceremony, an annual summer event to honor those who were impacted by nuclear weapons in Hiroshima, Nagasaki, and all over the world.

• • • ● • ● • ● • •

SHIVI AGARWAL holds a master's in management and has years of experience in human resources and learning and development. She currently works as a customer success manager with Kudos®. In her previous work tenure in Calgary, she helped 100+ clients transition from the oil and gas division to find employment in the tech sector. Shivi also runs a talk show in Calgary, The Startup Impact, as a side hustle. The saying she lives by is: "The only thing that matters is who you want to become and the price you are willing to pay to get there." www.linkedin.com/in/shivi-agarwal/

• • • ● • ● • • • •

DR. SWATI DHINGRA is a research coordinator at the University of Calgary. With her unique background in dentistry and oral medicine from India, she brings an exceptional blend of knowledge and expertise in academic, clinical and community research. She has contributed to several multi-disciplinary research projects at U of C and has been a part of community research projects with Alberta Health Services. Dr. Dhingra is passionate about social work and always looks for meaningful ways to give back to the community. She is also a trained classical Indian dancer and has an extraordinary love for music and travel.

• • • ● • ● • • • •

TATIANA OSHCHEPKOVA is a coordinator for the Canadian Network on Information and Security (CANIS) with the University of Calgary. She is responsible for the daily operations and strategic vision of the network through planning and coordinating interdisciplinary activities, events, and outreach initiatives. Previously, she worked in various administrative roles in both business and non-profit sectors, including coordination of national and provincial research projects, educational programs, and employment services for the immigrant population in Calgary. Tatiana holds a bachelor's and master's in social work from the University of Calgary, and a B.Sc. from the Ural Federal University, Russia.

· · · ● · ● · · ·

VITA LEUNG is Canadian-born Chinese, a jook-sing in Cantonese. This sounds like "bamboo star" and translates to "no access at both ends." Raised in Scarborough, Ontario, she now lives in Scarboro, Calgary with her husband, her son, and Kitty the Toronto street cat. They live in a house built in 1929 that does not resemble Hong Kong in any way, except for the orchid collection. Vita sounds like her Chinese name, which means "abundance of virtue." She's Catholic and doesn't believe in Hong Kong superstitions.

· · · ● · ● · ● · ·

YELENA SEDOVA is a blogger and the founder of a cabinet making company. She has an engineering degree and worked in marketing and advertising for over 20 years. Born in Russia, raised in Kazakhstan, Yelena currently lives in Calgary, Alberta, with her husband and two children. She has suffered from migraines for over 35 years and has developed a comprehensive method for getting rid of headaches, which has saved her. She is currently writing a

book on this method, in the hopes that she can help others.
Instagram: @sedovayelena

• • • ●●•●●•• •

ZOONG NGUYEN was born in Saigon, Việt Nam, and came to Canada at the end of the Vietnam War. She has lived in Montréal and Ottawa and has been in Calgary since 2005, with her husband and puppy Azo. She's a retired bookkeeper and graphic designer. With her two daughters now grown, Zoong dedicates her time to her art projects. She has always liked writing personal stories, and during the first COVID-19 lockdown, she started her memoir of life as a new Canadian. She has used acrylic paints to tell parts of the story and has exhibited her works. www.Zoong.ca

• • • ●●•●●•• •

Manufactured by Amazon.ca
Bolton, ON

27488477R00131